The Tennis Handbook

A Marshall Edition
Conceived, edited, and designed by
Marshall Editions
The Old Brewery
6 Blundell Street
London N7 9BH
www.quarto.com

Published in the United States by Three Rivers Press, an imprint of the Crown Publishing
Group, a division of Random House, Inc., New York.
www.crownpublishing.com

Three Rivers Press and the Tugboat design are
registered trademarks of Random House, Inc.

Library of Congress Cataloging-in-Publication
Data is available upon request

Originated in Hong Kong by Modern Age
Printed in China by Midas Printing International Limited

ISBN 13: 978-0-307-33943-0
ISBN 10: 0-307-33943-2

Publisher: Richard Green
Commissioning editor: Claudia Martin
Art direction: Ivo Marloh
Project editor: Johanna Geary
Editorial and design: Hart McLeod
Production: Nikki Ingram

10 9 8 7 6 5 4 3 2 1

First U.S. Edition

The Tennis Handbook

A Complete Guide to Acing Your Game

SUE RICH

 THREE RIVERS PRESS · NEW YORK

INTRODUCTION

Tennis is a wonderful sport—a highly complex and fascinating game. It provides exercise, competition, and fun. It is a game you can play all your life.

I started playing tennis at school and soon became hooked on the game, wanting to improve and compete at the highest level that I could. My early role models, only seen on TV, were Margaret Court and Billie Jean King. My love of the sport has not waned since those days. I still get a real buzz from playing and hitting the ball, and achieve great satisfaction from helping others to fulfil their potential, whatever that may be.

I hope that this book will inspire you, not only to play but also to work on your game, so that you too can fulfil your potential and get as much fun and pleasure out of the sport of tennis as I have done. Perhaps you will become a champion from this modest beginning.

I can vouch for the fact that practice, practice, and more practice, aligned with physical training and dedication, will give you a chance to achieve a high level. But whatever you do, don't forget to enjoy the game. Importantly, too, remember that it is never too late to start.

One small point: the book has been written mainly for a right-handed player, so if you are left-handed just substitute left for right. The left-handed slice serve is a wicked delivery—keep working at it!

I sincerely hope that you will enjoy your participation in this wonderful game. Good luck with your tennis.

CONTENTS

ORIGINS AND HISTORY

Ancient beginnings

Tennis, as we know it today, has been through many trends and developments since its surprising beginnings.

Many experts cite the ancient Egyptians as the founders of the game we play today, because ball games played as part of religious ceremonies are depicted in wall carvings in Egyptian temples from as early as 1500 BC.

The French origin of "real tennis"

When the empire of the Moors spread to southern France in the 8th century AD, Christian monks adopted a simple version of the game, known as *la soule*. This involved hitting the ball to and fro, using bare hands or a stick.

The game was played so frequently in the monasteries of France that it was almost banned by the church for causing a distraction. However, the popularity of *la soule* among royalty and the nobility ensured its continued growth.

The more familiar structure of tennis, developed by the French, was known as *jeu de paume* ("game of the palm") and was similar to squash in that it was played indoors and involved hitting a ball against a wall.

During the 15th century, the most basic rackets were introduced. French players

THE HIGH BORNE PRINCE IAMES DVKE of YORKE

Horseracing may be the sport of kings, but this didn't stop English and French kings playing real tennis. Above, **King James II** (then the Duke of York) enjoys the game in the 1600s.

would begin the game by shouting *tenez!* (meaning "play!"), the phrase that eventually gave rise to the name tennis. Its royal patronage led to its full name of real or royal tennis.

Real tennis emerged with the same fashionable status in England—becoming recognized as the "sport of the kings." Henry VIII was a keen player and built a court at his palace in Hampton Court.

The game continued to spread—to Spain, Holland, Germany, Switzerland, and Italy—but went into a decline in the 18th century because of changes caused by the French revolution and the Napoleonic wars.

To this day, real tennis is still enjoyed by dedicated enthusiasts. Henry VIII's Hampton Court is still used for public attraction and competitive games, as are a variety of other venues all over the world.

This **real tennis court** shows its medieval origins.

Lawn tennis

After a decline in the 18th century, the prosperity of Victorian 19th-century Britain triggered new developments in tennis. Wealthy people built private tennis courts, and the first clubs began to emerge.

The development of lawn tennis (a term coined by British statesman Arthur Balfour) enabled the game to break from its confinement to royalty and the nobility, because the upper classes could now enjoy tennis in their gardens. As the trend gained pace, players also experimented with clay and concrete courts for a more vigorous game.

The establishment of tennis as an important competitive sport was accelerated when the game was recognized by the All England Croquet Club—a major competitive club at the time. Because of the growing popularity of tennis this croquet club was losing much of its public interest so it decided to offer tennis as well.

The rise of competitive tennis

To raise funds for its new game, the All England Croquet and Lawn Tennis Club launched its first tournament in 1877. Official rules were drawn up by a committee, and the first championships took place off Worple Road, Wimbledon.

At first, the only event held was "gentlemen's singles." In 1884, the tournament extended to include ladies' singles and gentlemen's doubles, then in 1913 the club introduced ladies' doubles and mixed doubles.

The excitement of the growth of Wimbledon gave the game of tennis, and its players, worldwide recognition. The first tennis "personalities" began to show their colors, the most impressive of which was William Renshaw, who won the championships title eight times between 1881 and 1889 and set a standard that remains unbeaten today.

In 1922, the Wimbledon championships moved to its present location, off Church Road, where it continues to be regarded as the most prestigious event in tennis. Alongside the French Open, the Australian Open, and the US Open, the Wimbledon championships is one of the Grand Slam events of the tennis year.

William Renshaw playing against Herbert Lawford in an all-comers match prior to the final at **Wimbledon.** In the early years of the championships, players had to compete in the all-comers knock-out before gaining the opportunity to challenge the reigning champion.

THE LAWN TENNIS CHAMPIONSHIP MEETING AT WIMBLEDON—THE FIFTH ROUND OF THE ALL COMERS' MATCH

A COMPETITIVE SPORT

Tennis at the Olympics

Because it had become established as a competitive sport, tennis was included in the original nine events that comprised the first Olympic Games in Athens in 1896. The game was restricted to male competitors at first—as was the entire Olympic tournament. John Boland of Ireland was the first Olympic tennis champion. When women's tennis was introduced, some four years later, stars such as Charlotte Cooper (the first female champion), Laurie Doherty, Suzanne Lenglen, and Helen Wills Moody emerged into the spotlight of fame.

Tennis continued at the Olympics until it was withdrawn in 1924. The (then) International Lawn Tennis Federation had been dissatisfied with their treatment by the International Olympic Committee, who at the time refused their involvement in the overall organization of the Games and upheld an unreasonable request that Wimbledon should not be held in any Olympic year.

Following a long and determined campaign, a highly successful demonstration tennis event was included in the 1984 Olympics in Los Angeles. Steffi Graf and

Suzanne Lenglen's appearances in the Olympic Games gave her greater prominence.

Stefan Edberg, stars of this show, also led the way when tennis was welcomed back into the Olympic Games at Seoul in 1988. The authorities could not deny the popularity of the tennis stars involved, or the public interest in the game.

The Olympics continue to give a limelight to the most dominant tennis stars, and this exposure at international level is one of the factors that has fed the commercial status of the game.

The modern era

The 20th century saw the development of the game from the pastime of kings into a global sport played and viewed by millions.

The Davis Cup, an opportunity for the world's best to compete against each other, began in 1900 and has since produced memorable tennis moments fuelled by national pride. International expansion continued; 1905 saw the first Australian Open and 1928 the first staging of the French Open at Roland Garros, its famous home. With Wimbledon and the US Open, these tournaments form the Grand Slam. Interest in the women's game also grew, with the French player Suzanne Lenglen leading the way with her 1920 Wimbledon triple crown of ladies' singles, ladies' doubles, and mixed doubles.

World War II made the continuation of normal tennis business impossible, with Wimbledon, the French Open, and the Australian Open all put on hold. Wimbledon itself saw action when a bomb landed on the Center Court; fortunately there was no loss of life, only 1,200 seats! After 1945, designer Teddy Tinling shocked the tennis world with his dress for American Gertrude "Gussy" Moran, her lace-trimmed knickers prompting a debate in the British Parliament.

Tennis today is a **huge marketplace** attracting manufacturers, sponsors, and a range of service suppliers. The young are a particular target.

AN INTERNATIONAL GAME

The **impact of television** on all sports has been enormous; tennis is no exception. Today's top players are seen by millions of viewers around the world.

Such was the growing interest in the game that a more organized tour was inevitable. A movement started by American Jack Kramer in 1950 culminated in the "Open Era" of tennis from 1968; all tennis players, regardless of professional or amateur status, could compete in the same tennis tournaments.

Today's professionals circumnavigate the globe several times a year competing in various tours: the Association of Tennis Professionals (ATP) and Women's Tennis Association (WTA) for the top players, the Federation and Davis Cups, the Masters Series and, of course, those all-important Grand Slams. Kramer's developments included, in 1970, the introduction of a points system leading to the distribution of prize money at the end of the season, a contribution recognized in 1972 through his appointment as the first Executive Director

of the ATP, the governing body of tennis to this day. Controversy hit Wimbledon in 1973 when the ATP boycotted the championships following the suspension of Yugoslav Nikki Pilic.

1970 also saw the introduction of the tie-break, an invention by Jimmy Van Allen to curtail overly long sets. Largely successful, it failed in the 1985 Wimbledon encounter involving Gunnarson/Mortenson and Frawley/Pecci with a 26–24 tie-break.

The world's best players today enjoy celebrity status, attracting advertising contracts from multi-national companies and creating second careers. Monica Seles and Andre Agassi in the restaurant business, and Serena Williams (along with Tiger Woods and Joe Montana) in fashion are typical.

Technical innovation has emerged to meet the changing demands of the sport. Yellow tennis balls (1972) made the speeding ball more visible to cameras (color broadcasts began in 1967) and to spectators. Changes in racket construction and the raising of player fitness levels have resulted in a game dominated by power, exemplified by American Andy Roddick's 153 mph serve, recorded by the on-court speed gun. The "Cyclops" machine had already been introduced, a rather unreliable gadget designed to "bleep" when a service was long.

Many claim the game is now too fast and powerful and lacks the finesse of former times. Suggestions to reduce the impact of the "big hitters" have included a return to wooden rackets, lengthening the court, increasing the size and reducing the pressure of the balls, and allowing only one serve into a narrower service area to reduce angles. All have so far been resisted, reflecting a determination to retain this great game intact for all, be they recreational player or world beater.

The modern game! **Serena Williams** at the 2004 US Open playing in an outfit she had designed herself and could market through her own fashion line.

DEVELOPMENT OF EQUIPMENT

The tennis ball

The familiar yellow ball used in tennis matches today has been through many developments since the first games of tennis were played. Although real/royal tennis and lawn tennis are similar, the types of ball traditionally used are very different.

Real tennis balls typically consisted of a stitched leather or cloth casing, stuffed with horsehair, rags, or something similar.

Lawn tennis, however, required a softer ball so as not to damage the grass. This became possible after the introduction of vulcanized "India rubber," which was invented by Charles Goodyear during the 1850s.

At first the lawn tennis ball was simply a solid rubber sphere. However, the durability of the ball was later improved by a cloth casing stitched into the rubber. Then the ball was made hollow and pressured with gas, which increased its bounce.

Originally, lawn tennis balls were either black or white in color, depending on the surface in play. It wasn't until 1972 that the International Tennis Federation introduced yellow balls on the basis that they were more visible for television viewing. Wimbledon, however, did not adopt the yellow ball until 1986. Today, the yellow ball is universal.

The tennis racket

The rackets typical of today's tennis have also come a long way since the early use of sticks, gloves, or even bare hands to hit the ball in the course of a game.

Wooden rackets

In the 1500s, the first wooden tennis rackets began to emerge. They consisted of a wooden frame laced with strings made from sheep's intestines. It is thought that the first proper racket was actually invented in Italy in 1583.

By the late 1800s, the racket head had grown to a size that remained constant (although varying in shape and materials) until the 1970s.

There were only minor changes to rackets in the late 19th and early 20th century. Although wooden rackets did improve during

These **real tennis balls**—as they are called today—are the forerunner of the modern lawn tennis ball.

This **lawn tennis set** from the early part of the 20th century includes old-style wooden rackets.

this century, with advances in "laminating technology" (using thin layers of wood glued together) and in strings, players were disadvantaged by the weight of the wood and the small size of the racket heads—factors that would not improve until new materials were explored.

Metal rackets

The first metal racket existed as early as 1889, but failed to surpass the popularity of the wooden racket. This changed in 1967, when Wilson Sporting Goods introduced the "T2000"—the first real step away from the use of wood in tennis rackets.

A variety of old **wooden tennis rackets.**

The T2000 was the steel racket first popularized by Jimmy Connors, who used it in a Wimbledon final—against the wooden racket of Bjorn Borg—to devastating effect. This was probably the first time that technology was seen as a major factor in the game's development.

A series of subsequent innovations has seen the graphite racket, with anti-vibration devices, dominate the game. It was John McEnroe, using the (then) incredibly light 12.5oz (355g) racket, who first championed graphite rackets in the 1980s. Since then a host of variations, including titanium and fiberglass, have been tried. With the game enjoying worldwide popularity, the next big thing in racket design could be a real money spinner.

Modern **graphite rackets** and tournament balls.

THE BIG TOURNAMENTS

The Grand Slam

In the modern game the four "majors" or Grand Slam events—comprising the Australian, French, and US Opens, and the Wimbledon championships—are those that receive the most attention. Players plan their event diaries in order to be at peak fitness for these tournaments.

The idea of a Grand Slam was first discussed in the 1930s, when it looked like Australian Jack Crawford would win the four tournaments in one year. Sadly, he failed at the last hurdle (the US Open). Very few players have achieved, or are ever likely to win, the Grand Slam, especially since they are now played on different surfaces: Two types of hard court in Australia and the US, clay in France, and grass at Wimbledon.

The Australian Open, which is also known as the Grand Slam of Asia Pacific, is held in Melbourne in mid-January and is traditionally the season's opener. The competition is played on a hard surface and has been characterized by very high temperatures. It was first held in 1905.

The French Open, played at the Roland Garros courts in Paris, started as a one-day tournament in 1891. The competition flourished during the heyday of French tennis in the first half of the 20th century. It began to accept non-French competitors in 1925 and became an open competition in 1968.

The Wimbledon championships claim to be the oldest tennis tournament in the world—first staged in 1877. Tradition still

Play on an outside court at the **Australian Open**.

Wimbledon during the championship fortnight. The Center Court will have a roof by the 2009 championships.

plays a large part in the championships. Some players don't like the competition because the matches are played on grass, but many others say grass is their favorite surface.

The tennis season's last major is the US Open at Flushing Meadows in Queens, New York. It was held on grass until 1974, moved to clay from 1975 to 1977, and then became a hard court tournament. Large and patriotic crowds characterize floodlit matches, especially in the 20,000-plus seater Arthur Ashe court. With the need to provide excitement on the court, the US Open was the first major to adopt the tie-break.

The Arthur Ashe court is filled with noisy crowds during the US Open.

The Tennis Masters Cup

Alongside the Grand Slams (open to both men and women) is a series of Association of Tennis Professionals (ATP) competitions for men. These are staged around the world and allow players not only to win titles and prize money but also to gather points and a world ranking. At the end of the season the Tennis Masters Cup puts the world's eight top-ranked players into competition. Played indoors, the competition is staged in a different country—on a different continent—every year.

Alongside the men's events is the Women's Tennis Association (WTA) tour.

Representing your country

Most tennis is for individuals—or pairs of players. However, there are a few occasions where a player can represent his or her country. Most notable are the team events—the Davis Cup for men and Federation Cup (known as the Fed Cup) for women. The cups are competed for in regional zones, then the leading teams play to qualify for the annual final. Although some of the top players do not compete, these competitions remain the focus for team events in tennis and they still retain the capacity to engender great patriotic support.

In addition, players can also represent their countries at the Olympic Games. Once the preserve of amateurs, playing at the Olympics was often considered the peak of a player's career. Tennis at the Olympics ceased as the Open Era in the sport developed (see page 12). Today, somewhat controversially, professionals have the opportunity, once every four years at the Games, to win gold medals instead of money.

TENNIS GREATS

Bill Tilden

Bill Tilden (1893–1953)

US star "Big Bill" Tilden dominated the men's game in the 1920s and 1930s with seven US championships, participation in seven Davis Cup victories, and a wealth of victories in the US and Europe. It is said that during the period of his dominance he even lost an occasional game or set, just to keep it interesting!

Born into wealth, Tilden moved in celebrity circles and enjoyed the fame the game brought him. He helped move tennis from a genteel game to one where physicality and mental toughness were important. He certainly played to win and used his huge serve as a key weapon. If his serves did not bring immediate success he would prefer to rally from the baseline until his strength and accuracy wore down his opponent.

Like a number of top players of his age, Tilden had to make the difficult decision to turn professional—to give up competing for prestigious titles and play for the money that fans were prepared to pay. Among a wealth of positives from his period in the game, Tilden may also be remembered as one of the first athletes to be accepted as a homosexual.

Suzanne Lenglen (1899–1938)

It was illness that brought Frenchwoman Suzanne Lenglen into the game—her father thought tennis might help her overcome asthma—an illness that brought about her untimely death. She died of pernicious anaemia at the age of 39.

Lenglen won more than 20 singles and doubles titles at Wimbledon and the French championships and was an Olympic gold medallist. Of her 81 singles championship successes, seven were achieved without losing a game.

Although all her major victories were achieved in Europe, she was the first truly international female tennis star. After World War I there was great clamor for her to play in the US. Her first visit, in 1921, was blighted by illness. Her second, as a

professional nearly six years later, was a triumph. Interest was enormous in the French star who dressed "immodestly" and took brandy between games. However, it was her quick feet and great ball placement that allowed her to dominate the women's game for nearly a decade.

This national French heroine turned to coaching and writing after retirement from tournament play.

Suzanne Lenglen

Helen Wills Moody (1905–1998)

Helen Wills Moody won 31 major titles in both singles and doubles and two gold medals at the 1924 Olympics in Paris. Between 1927 and 1938 she won eight Wimbledon singles titles, losing only one match in the process. Interestingly, Wills Moody was equally successful, and popular, in the US and Europe and was part of the process of making tennis a truly international game.

19

TENNIS GREATS

On court she lived up to her nickname of "Little Miss Poker Face," rarely giving anything away. The public were captivated by her "match of the century" against Suzanne Lenglen in 1926 in Monte Carlo. Lenglen, coming to the end of her career, won the match 6–3 8–6 and promptly turned professional, paving the way for Wills Moody's supremacy in the amateur game.

Alongside her tennis achievements, Wills Moody exhibited her paintings, wrote a novel, and left $10 million to her old university (Berkeley, California) for medical research.

Perry was the son of a British Labour MP and had many friendships with Hollywood stars of the time. Such friendships probably proved very useful as he launched his successful sports clothing lines. Today, Perry's statue stands outside the Wimbledon courts, playing what appears to be his characteristic right-handed approach shot.

Fred Perry

Helen Wills Moody

Fred Perry (1909–1995)

Englishman Fred Perry's 1935 French Open success meant he was the first player to win all four Grand Slam titles. His final total was eight, reached in the following year. Perry's three-in-a-row Wimbledon successes—the third final won inside 40 minutes in 1936—made him the last "home" player to win the championship and he is thus a British legend.

Perry was not always that popular. He "unsportingly" looked for weaknesses in his opponents and preyed on them. Sometimes he even argued with court officials and tennis administrators.

Don Budge (1915–2000)

In 1938, Californian Don Budge became the first player to win all four Grand Slam tournaments in the same year—part of a run of six consecutive Grand Slam wins. He then turned professional! Competing against this tall, slim man who had a great serve was compared to playing against a brick wall. Although not the most elegant or stylish player, Budge did appear to return every shot.

The timing of his career, however, was not great. He was reaching his peak as World War II began. In 1941, in the absence of world competition but still only 26 years old, he retired to concentrate on business interests. He also served in the US air force.

During his career Budge played a large number of head-to-head matches against other top players.

In a sport saturated with exciting matches, people still talk about Budge's winning 1937 Davis Cup encounter with German Gottfried Von Cramm. Budge won the fifth set 8–6, having trailed by two sets, 4–1 in the last.

Connolly's achievements are remarkable, perhaps more so considering that she changed from left- to right-handed, believing that left-handed players could not win major events. After her enforced retirement she became extremely popular as a commentator and writer. She tragically died young.

Don Budge

Maureen Connolly

Roy Emerson (b.1936)

Australian Roy Emerson was probably the best player in the world at the time the major championships were opened to all-comers. His total of 12 singles and 16 men's doubles titles—nine on home territory—in Grand Slam events is remarkable. Many of the top players were, at the time, playing professionally.

Emerson's particular asset was his strength. He trained excessively hard, was a strong serve-and-volley player, and was more likely to win a match the longer it went on. In a re-matched 1965 Australian final, Emerson beat fellow Australian Fred Stolle in five sets, having lost the first two 9–7 6–2. This was part of a five-year winning sequence (1963–67) in the event.

Rod Laver (b.1938)

Australian Rod Laver's achievement of winning all four Grand Slams in a single year twice, in 1962 and 1969, sets him at the

Maureen Connolly (1934–1969)

In 1953 American Maureen Connolly, "Little Mo" as she was universally known, won all four Grand Slam singles titles: Wimbledon, and the open championships of the US, France, and Australia. She was only 18 and the first woman—and second person—ever to achieve this feat. In total Connolly won all nine Grand Slam singles in which she competed, gaining her first US title at the age of 16. Sadly, however, her career will always be remembered for what might have been, rather than what she actually achieved. In 1954, while out horseriding (her first sporting love), she was involved in an accident. She broke her leg badly and never competed again.

TENNIS GREATS

pinnacle of the men's game. Statistics alone are unhelpful in measuring his succuss because he spent a number of years as a professional when most major tournaments were only for amateurs. In his first full "open" season Laver had a 106–16 win ratio in singles matches and was the first player to accrue $1 million in prize money.

He was the first of a number of Australians to reach the very top in world tennis, and he helped his country win the Davis Cup in four consecutive years, from 1959. He was also on the winning team in 1973, when Australia beat the US 5–0.

Left-handed Laver, known as "Rocket" on account of his powerful ground shots, is also credited with perfecting and popularizing the topspin shot.

Rod Laver

Margaret Court (b.1942)
Margaret Court was the victor at 11 Australian Opens, at the US and French Opens on five occasions, and at Wimbledon on three occasions. In all she won 62 Grand Slam titles—24 singles, 19 doubles, and 19 mixed. She gained 17 singles titles in one year alone (1971). Although statistics alone do not make a player great, these remarkable figures hint at the pre-eminence of one of the world's greatest players.

A strong serve and forceful forehand were Court's main weapons on all surfaces. Never flamboyant on or off court, her progress in the game was relentless, not spectacular. Her achievement was particularly noteworthy when one considers that she was competing with Billie Jean King through much of her career and took significant breaks from the game to have her children. Her 14–12 11–9 Wimbledon final victory against King in 1970 is remembered as one of the best women's matches ever. She retired in 1977.

Billie Jean King (b.1943)
American Billie Jean King had a brilliant record in women's tennis, comprising 12 Grand Slam titles among more than 60 major singles successes. She won 39 Grand Slam titles in all. King was an athlete in every sense of the word: fit, strong, and very determined on court. Her rivalry with Margaret Court produced some of the greatest matches ever seen in women's tennis.

More than this, perhaps, King may be remembered for the way she helped transform women's tennis. She was largely responsible for creating the women's tour and persuading sponsors and organizers to pay much greater prize money. She also won the noted "battle of the sexes" against self-publicist and one-time Wimbledon champion Bobby Riggs, winning in straight sets in front of more than 50 million television viewers.

Although nobody doubted her altruism—King was also a great supporter of junior tennis—she also benefited from her campaigning. In 1971 she became the first woman athlete to win more than $100,000 in prize money.

Billie Jean King

John Newcombe (b.1944)

Along with Rod Laver, Tony Roche, Roy Emerson, and Ken Rosewall, John Newcombe helped keep Australia at the forefront of world tennis in the 1960s and early 1970s. He won seven Grand Slam singles titles and 17 doubles, and was world number one in 1970, 1971, and 1973.

Newcombe's fast-paced serve-and-volley game made him exciting to watch and difficult to play against; it also made him a great doubles player. He took risks on court, especially with ambitious (often winning) second serves.

Jimmy Connors (b.1952)

Left-handed American star Jimmy Connors reached the top of the world rankings in July 1974 and stayed there for more than three years. In his career he was world number one for a total of 263 weeks. Among more than 100 successes were his five US Open singles titles.

What made Connors extra special was his intense desire to win. Opponents knew that he would never give up. He matched aggression with doggedness, and he enjoyed all surfaces and feared nobody.

Connors frequently challenged the status quo. He fell out with the Association of Tennis Professionals and was one of the first top players to move from wooden to metal rackets—not a universally popular move at the time. The latter part of his career was enlivened by a fierce rivalry with John McEnroe.

Chris Evert (b.1954)

Chris Evert's father was a professional coach and helped her achieve exceptional success as a youngster. In her first year at the US Open, in 1971, she reached the semi-final before losing to Billie Jean King.

The American "ice maiden" was particularly strong on clay, where her baseline accuracy and intense concentration led her to a record 125 consecutive victories from 1973 to 1979. In all she won 18 Grand Slam singles titles, including seven French Opens. Remarkably, in her first seven years as a professional, Evert never lost two matches in a row.

Her achievements are all the more extraordinary when one considers that her career overlapped considerably with that of Martina Navratilova. They met 80 times—Navratilova holding a 43–37 advantage. Evert retired in 1989.

Jimmy Connors

Chris Evert

TENNIS GREATS

Bjorn Borg

Martina Navratilova

Bjorn Borg (b.1956)

"Ice man," as Bjorn Borg was nicknamed, was famous for his unblinking concentration and coldly consistent baseline play. From 1973 to his early retirement in 1981, he won five Wimbledon titles in a row and six French Open titles, including four in a row. Although Borg was able to play equally well on all surfaces, he competed only once at the Australian Open and underachieved at the US Open, where he claimed he didn't like playing under floodlights. His Wimbledon finals against John McEnroe in 1980 and 1981 were two of the most fascinating games of tennis in the modern era.

Borg very much reflected his era, and his long hair tied back was a huge hit with young female fans. He is credited with making the game much more popular in Scandinavia; several other top Swedes followed him into the professional game.

Many believed that Borg retired too soon. An attempted return to the game in the early 1990s was a failure, although he later resumed old rivalries on the masters circuit.

Martina Navratilova (b.1956)

Left-handed Martina Navratilova was born in (then) Czechoslovakia and defected as a top player to the US in 1975, where she proceeded to win at the highest level for 30 more years!

She attempted to dominate opponents with a strong serve-and-volley game. This was particularly effective on fast courts, and she won nine women's singles finals on the grass of Wimbledon. She also excelled at doubles and, with Pam Shriver, notched an incredible 109 match-winning streak. In all, Navratilova won 18 Grand Slam singles titles and held a record in the women's game of 74 singles victories in a row.

Her remarkable achievements ensured that she dominated the game in the early and mid-1980s. She won her last Wimbledon trophy, the mixed doubles, in 2003. They say great players need great rivals. Navratilova had two: Chris Evert in her early career and Steffi Graf later. Outside of the game, Martina worked extensively for animal and children's charities.

John McEnroe (b.1959)

At one point in his early career, American John McEnroe was in danger of being known more for his bad behavior and lack of respect for tradition than for his considerable skill. Both officialdom and his opponents found him hard to handle.

There is no doubt that McEnroe made tennis more interesting, bringing in a wider audience who thrilled to his powerful play and petulant personality. His aggressive left-handed game saw him win 77 singles titles, including seven Grand Slams, between 1978 and 1992. He enjoyed rivalries with other top players of the time, notably Jimmy Connors and Bjorn Borg, both of whom he met in classic Wimbledon finals. McEnroe's most remarkable year was 1984, when he had an 82–3 singles record and won a career-high 13 singles tournaments, including his third Wimbledon and fourth US Open titles.

It should never be forgotten that he also won 78 doubles tournaments—a testament to his extraordinary stamina.

After retirement, and perhaps mellowing a little, McEnroe became a very popular and respected commentator as well as a fierce competitor on the masters circuit.

John McEnroe

TENNIS GREATS

Andre Agassi

Steffi Graf

Andre Agassi (b.1970)

Andre Agassi has long been recognized as one of the game's most entertaining players. At the age of three he was deemed a tennis prodigy, and he was still competing for major championships at the age of 35. His father was an Olympic boxer.

From childhood stardom, Agassi turned professional in 1986 and finished in the world's top 10 for 16 of the 20 years that he was a professional. His career included 59 singles titles, and he was one of only three men to win all four Grand Slam titles in the Open Era. In addition, Agassi won an Olympic gold medal in Atlanta in 1996.

In terms of technique, Agassi based his game on some of the simplest shots in the book. He might appear easy to copy, but he possessed an unbelievable ability to take the ball early. His return of serve—perfected with a compact backswing—was perhaps his most damaging shot.

Agassi was not only a first-rate tennis professional but also did a tremendous amount for charity. The Andre Agassi Charitable Foundation raised nearly $40 million, primarily for underprivileged children. This American tennis player was a true ambassador for his sport.

Steffi Graf (b.1969)

Was German Steffi Graf or Australian Margaret Court the greatest-ever player? Graf won 22 Grand Slam singles titles, beginning in 1987. In 1988 she became the only woman to win the "Golden Slam," all four Grand Slams plus an Olympic gold medal. She was world number one for more than 350 weeks. Above all, Graf was a fantastic athlete with an incredible forehand drive and an excellently controlled backhand slice. She was equally strong on all surfaces.

Off-court events affected her later career. A trying relationship with her father/coach Peter Graf contributed to poor form, and her domination ended when challenged by Monica Seles. Later, when Seles was stabbed by a Graf "fan," the German rose to the top again.

Injury forced a slightly premature retirement in 1999. Graf married US tennis star Andre Agassi in 2001.

Pete Sampras (b.1971)

Finishing number one in the world rankings for six successive years—and scooping a record 14 Grand Slam singles titles—probably accounted for "Pistol Pete's" reputation as the greatest male tennis player ever. The fact

Pete Sampras

that he never won the French Open, nor was a flamboyant or outspoken champion, meant that some dispute the claim.

Greek-American Sampras won his first US Open when he was only 18, in 1990, and his last in 2002. Both matches were against Andre Agassi. It was the combination of Sampras' serve and all-round speed that gave him his nickname and his success. His second serve was often as deadly as his first, and he was credited with perfecting, if not inventing, the "slam-dunk" smash.

Sampras' achievement is all the more remarkable as it came at a time when there were other great players around—notably Andre Agassi—and when big rewards encouraged intense competition.

Venus (b.1980) and Serena (b.1981) Williams

Venus, and younger sister Serena, grew up in a low-rent, high-crime area of Los Angeles, California. Both sisters were playing in tournaments before their teens, coached mostly by their father, Richard, who taught himself tennis from a "how-to-play" book. Venus turned pro at 14 and quickly climbed the world rankings, making it to the US Open in 1997. It was Serena, however, who, in 1999, made the bigger headlines. She won the US Open, becoming the first African-American woman to claim a Grand Slam title in almost five decades. By 2002 Serena and Venus were numbers one and two in the world. The younger sister defeated her older sibling in the finals of the French Open, Wimbledon, and the US Open in that year.

Their similar and successful games have been largely based on strong ground strokes and powerful serves, but they are more than just tennis stars. They are also cultural icons with interests in a number of fields. Despite their obvious rivalry, the sisters have been consistently good friends, bound by their family and Church interests as much as by the "celebrity" lives they lead.

Roger Federer (b.1981)

It is rare for one player to be universally acknowledged as the best in the world, yet Swiss-born Roger Federer achieved that feat during the 2004/05 season. Admired by opponents and fans alike, Federer's brilliance on the court was matched by modesty and humanity off it. He moved rapidly toward the top of the game, reaching number one status in 2004. In that year he won 11 tournaments including three Grand Slams.

Federer's concentration was clearly a major plus in his game. By 2005 he had won 15 consecutive finals and possessed a winning streak on grass of 24 matches. For a long time he toured the world without a coach, and he relied on family and friends to manage his tennis affairs. His game was based on a range of qualities including speed, accuracy, confidence, and the ability to improvise when needed.

Like many great players Federer not only played all the classic shots but also produced a range of intuitive—possibly unreproducible—shots. By 2006, the game of tennis waited to see just how dominant, on the court and in the record books, Federer was to become.

Roger Federer

The tennis stars of yesterday have marked their place in the game's history. But there will be more great names as time moves on. We may be watching a Suzanne Lenglen or Don Budge of the future right now. There are many contenders for the title of "all-time great"—Maria Sharapova is just one.

Maria Sharapova (b.1987)

Russian-born Maria Sharapova was one of several exciting Russians to emerge onto the tennis scene in 2004. She won Wimbledon that year and, later, the WTA tour championships. She was world number one in mid-2005.

Sharapova started playing tennis in Russia at the age of four, and at seven years old she and her father went to Nick Bollettieri's Academy in Florida, USA. This entailed a difficult two-year separation from her mother, but the family was eventually re-united and viewed this as a sacrifice worth making.

Sharapova has tremendous desire and hunger for the game, no doubt helped by her background and her determination to succeed. Her height, over 6ft (1.8m), enables her to generate pace and find the angles on the serve. She also has tremendous reach, keeping a lot of balls in play that other players might not.

She is one of many players for whom a glittering future is predicted. Sharapova's longevity in the game will depend on her continued fitness and competitive hunger—and perhaps memories of what she gave up to reach her current standing.

RULES AND SCORING

Properly **qualified umpires** help players keep score, can adjudicate on line calls, and control the players and crowd, although the majority of non-professional tennis is played without such help.

Tennis may look simple when you are watching a professional match, yet in fact it is a complex game with detailed rules.

The court

The measurements and markings of a tennis court are universally standardized. They cater for singles games involving two players as well as doubles, for four players:

• the court is rectangular in shape and is 78ft (23.77m) long and 27ft (8.23m) wide for singles matches;
• for doubles matches the court is 36ft (10.97m) wide;
• the court is divided across the middle by the net, which is 3ft (0.914m) high at the center and 3ft 6ins (1.07m) at the edge, and attached to two posts;
• for a doubles match, the posts are 3ft (0.914m) outside the court on each side (the net is suspended on a cord between them);
• the lines at the ends of the court are called baselines, and the lines at the side of the court are called sidelines (or tramlines);
• the service lines are marked 21ft (6.40m) from the net and lie parallel to it;
• the area between the service line and the net forms the service boxes, which are equally divided by the center service line;
• the center of each baseline is divided by the center mark.

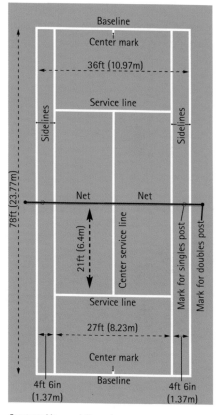

Court markings and dimensions.

The game

The game starts with the serve. The choice of server or receiver is decided by a coin toss before the warm-up starts. If you win the toss you are entitled to one of the following privileges:

• to decide whether you want to be the server or receiver in the first game;
• to choose the end of the court from which you will begin the match;
• to ask that your opponent makes the choice.

Once these decisions have been made, there is a maximum of five minutes in which to warm up, before the actual game begins.

The server must start with both feet behind the baseline, to the right of the center mark. A good serve is one that crosses the net and

lands in the diagonally opposite service box, provided you have served from the correct position and have not foot-faulted. The ball is still in if it touches any of the lines enclosing the service box.

The most common fault with the serve is the foot fault. Your serve is invalid if you:
• walk or run while serving (slight movements are allowed);
• cross the baseline with either foot before hitting the ball;
• touch the area outside the imaginary extension of the sideline with either foot;
• touch the imaginary extension of the center mark with either foot.

RULES AND SCORING

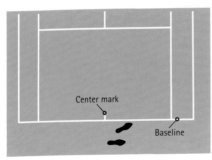

Foot position when serving

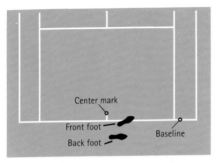

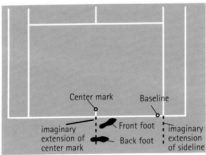

Examples of foot faults

If you make any of these mistakes the umpire will call "foot fault."

The umpire will also call a fault if:
• your ball does not land in the correct box;
• you attempt to hit the ball and miss it;
• your served ball touches a permanent fixture, singles stick, or net post before it hits the ground;
• your served ball touches you, or your partner (in doubles), or anything you or your partner are wearing or carrying.

If you serve a fault you are allowed a second serve. If you fault again on your second serve, the point is lost.

A LET

A "let" is called when your served ball hits the net before hitting the ground, but still falls into the correct service box. A let can also be called if you serve to the receiver when they are not ready or if players are distracted, e.g. by a rolling ball or crowd noise.

When a let is called, the score does not change. If it is called on your first serve, you are allowed two more attempts, and if it is called on your second serve you are allowed one more attempt.

Winning points

Once the serve has been made, the game is all about the various ways in which you can win and lose points.

Here are some of the ways you can win points in tennis:
• serving an unreturnable first or second serve—an "ace";
• hitting the ball in such a way that it bounces twice in your opponent's court before your opponent can hit it;
• forcing your opponent to make an error, such as to hit the ball into the net or out of court;
• if your opponent serves two faults in a row—a double fault;
• if your opponent hits the ball before it passes over the net.

If the ball **double bounces**, the point is lost.

Losing points

Unfortunately, there seem to be more ways to lose points than to win them:

• the ball is allowed to bounce only once on the ground before it is returned over the net. If you let the ball bounce twice, you lose the point immediately;

• if the ball in play hits a permanent fixture, or another object outside the court, you lose the point;

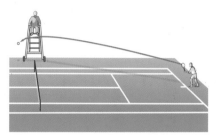

If the ball **hits a "permanent fixture,"** the point is lost.

• if you volley the ball from behind the baseline and make a bad return, you lose the point, so try not to volley from behind the baseline (if you do and the ball is in then the point continues);

• if you stand outside the baseline and touch the ball before it bounces, thinking the ball was out, you will lose the point. The ball must always bounce before an "out" decision can be made;

• if you, including your racket, whether in your hand or not, or anything that you are wearing or carrying touches any part of the net or your opponent's court at any

time while the ball is in play; you will lose the point;

• you cannot play the ball before it crosses the net except, for example, on a very windy day when your opponent hits a drop shot and the ball rebounds back over the net onto their side. You are then allowed to reach over and play the ball, provided you do not touch the net;

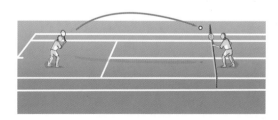

If the ball is **played before it crosses the net**, the point is lost.

RULES AND SCORING

• you are not allowed to carry or catch the ball in play deliberately on your racket or touch it with the racket more than once, unless you strike it twice in one stroke;
• the ball is not allowed to touch you or anything you wear or carry except your racket—if it does you will lose the point;
• you cannot throw your racket at the ball in an attempt to get the ball back into play—if you do you will lose the point.

There are some more obscure ways of losing a point, which may be called if you have an umpire:
• you are not allowed to change the shape of your racket deliberately and materially when the ball is in play;
• you cannot distract your opponent while he or she is making a shot, or cause any hindrance to him or her.

Good returns

There are several types of shot that, while you might expect them to be disallowed, are actually "good returns." These are:
• if the ball touches the net, net posts/singles sticks, cord, or metal cable, strap, or band and passes over them and hits the ground in the correct court, then the ball is allowed to continue in play;
• if you return the ball outside the net posts, either above or below the level of the top of the net, the return is allowed provided it lands in the court;
• if the ball passes underneath the net cord (between the singles sticks and adjacent net post) without touching any part of the net itself, and lands in the correct court, it is allowed;
• if your racket passes over the net after hitting the ball on your side of the net, and if the ball bounces on the ground in the correct court, it is allowed;
• if your opponent leaves a ball lying on the court and you hit it with the ball in play, the rally may continue provided the correct ball is returned into play. However, if a ball rolls onto your court from another court during play then the point is replayed.

Scoring

The tennis scoring system can be quite confusing if you are a beginner, because it does not follow a strictly logical pattern. The present system of scoring was derived from real tennis, where points now named fifteen, thirty, and forty represented the minutes on a "scoring clock."

Games

A tennis match is composed of games, which in turn make up "sets." At the beginning of each game, the score stands at "love—all" (0-0). The server's score is always called first.

The standard sequence of points is as follows:

no point	—	"love"
first point	—	"15"
second point	—	"30"
third point	—	"40"
fourth point	—	"game"

The scoring system becomes more complicated when players reach equal scores. If both players are at "40" then the score is "deuce." After deuce, if you win the next point your score changes to "advantage." You then must win the next point in order to avoid returning to deuce. A player must win two points in a row to win the game after a deuce score has been reached.

Let's consider an imaginary game:
• you win the coin toss and elect to serve first;
• you win the first point so the score becomes 15–0 ("fifteen—love");
• you lose the next point, so the score changes to 15–15 ("fifteen—all");
• you win the next point, so the score is 30–15 ("thirty—fifteen");
• you win the next point, so the score is 40–15 ("forty—fifteen");
• you then serve an ace and thereby win the game.

Sets and matches
There are two ways in which to win a set:
• in an "advantage set" you must win six games as well as have a margin of two games over your opponent. If necessary, the set continues until you are two games ahead of your opponent: E.g., eight games to six;
• a "tie-break set" is played when you and your opponent both reach six games each. This variation is used in order to decide the winner of the set.

THE TIE-BREAK GAME

During the tie-break the points are scored: "zero," "one," "two," "three," etc. The first player to win seven points, with a margin of two points over their opponent, wins the game and set.

The player whose turn it is to serve does so for the first point in the tie-break from the deuce court. Following this, players serve for two points at a time until the end of the game. After every six points players change ends.

At the end of the tie-break and therefore the set, the score is 7–6 so you then change ends, because the tie-break counts as one game. The person who received first in the tie-break then serves for the first game in the next set.

A match is usually the best of three sets (the first player to gain two sets wins), although in Grand Slam events the men's singles matches are played as the best of five sets (the first player to gain three sets wins). Some matches involve a tie-break in all sets, whereas in others the final set is played as an advantage set.

Ensure you know what scoring system you are using before you begin a match.

BREAKS AND CHANGING ENDS

At the end of the first game in a set, players should swap over to play from the opposite ends of the court. This end change occurs after every odd-numbered game of each set.

If the score at the end of the first set is 6–4, the players are entitled to a two-minute break, but they must return to the same end that they were playing from in the previous game. Players are allowed a maximum of 20 seconds in between each point played and 90 seconds at each change of ends. However, after the first game of each set and during a tie-break, play is continuous and players change ends without a break. Players are allowed breaks to attend to injuries.

HINT

Tennis scoring means you may lose a battle (game or set) but not the war. You are given several fresh starts in a match.

COMPETITIONS

The competitive experience of tennis can be a little daunting, so start by getting involved with your local club tournament. If you are successful you can progress to a district or open tournament, where you will have the chance to play against different opposition and on different types of court. Tournaments can follow various formats.

Kim Clijsters holds aloft the US Open championship trophy in 2005.

Traditional or knock-out draw
This is the format used in all Grand Slam events. The highest-ranked players are "seeded" and placed in predetermined places in the draw. If you lose you are "knocked out" of the tournament.

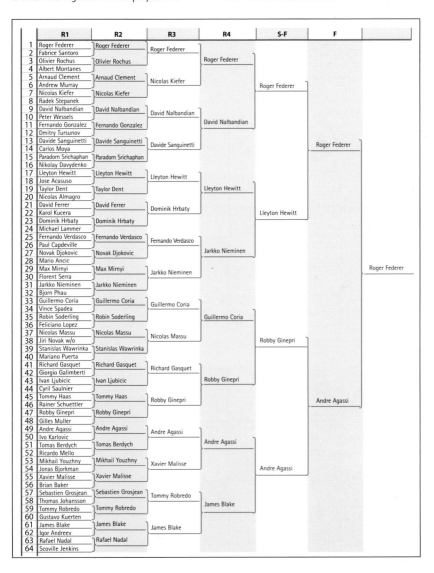

	R1	R2	R3	R4	S-F	F
1	Roger Federer	Roger Federer				
2	Fabrice Santoro		Roger Federer			
3	Olivier Rochus	Olivier Rochus		Roger Federer		
4	Albert Montanes					
5	Arnaud Clement	Arnaud Clement			Roger Federer	
6	Andrew Murray		Nicolas Kiefer			
7	Nicolas Kiefer	Nicolas Kiefer				
8	Radek Stepanek					
9	David Nalbandian	David Nalbandian				
10	Peter Wessels		David Nalbandian			
11	Fernando Gonzalez	Fernando Gonzalez		David Nalbandian		
12	Dmitry Tursunov					Roger Federer
13	Davide Sanguinetti	Davide Sanguinetti				
14	Carlos Moya		Davide Sanguinetti			
15	Paradorn Srichaphan	Paradorn Srichaphan				
16	Nikolay Davydenko					
17	Lleyton Hewitt	Lleyton Hewitt				
18	Jose Acasuso		Lleyton Hewitt			
19	Taylor Dent	Taylor Dent		Lleyton Hewitt		
20	Nicolas Almagro					
21	David Ferrer	David Ferrer			Lleyton Hewitt	
22	Karol Kucera		Dominik Hrbaty			
23	Dominik Hrbaty	Dominik Hrbaty				
24	Michael Lammer					
25	Fernando Verdasco	Fernando Verdasco				
26	Paul Capdeville		Fernando Verdasco			
27	Novak Djokovic	Novak Djokovic		Jarkko Nieminen		
28	Mario Ancic					
29	Max Mirnyi	Max Mirnyi				Roger Federer
30	Florent Serra		Jarkko Nieminen			
31	Jarkko Nieminen	Jarkko Nieminen				
32	Bjorn Phau					
33	Guillermo Coria	Guillermo Coria				
34	Vince Spadea		Guillermo Coria			
35	Robin Soderling	Robin Soderling		Guillermo Coria		
36	Feliciano Lopez					
37	Nicolas Massu	Nicolas Massu			Robby Ginepri	
38	Jiri Novak w/o		Nicolas Massu			
39	Stanislas Wawrinka	Stanislas Wawrinka				
40	Mariano Puerta					
41	Richard Gasquet	Richard Gasquet				
42	Giorgio Galimberti		Richard Gasquet			
43	Ivan Ljubicic	Ivan Ljubicic		Robby Ginepri		
44	Cyril Saulnier					
45	Tommy Haas	Tommy Haas			Andre Agassi	
46	Rainer Schuettler		Robby Ginepri			
47	Robby Ginepri	Robby Ginepri				
48	Gilles Muller					
49	Andre Agassi	Andre Agassi				
50	Ivo Karlovic		Andre Agassi			
51	Tomas Berdych	Tomas Berdych		Andre Agassi		
52	Ricardo Mello					
53	Mikhail Youzhny	Mikhail Youzhny			Andre Agassi	
54	Jonas Bjorkman		Xavier Malisse			
55	Xavier Malisse	Xavier Malisse				
56	Brian Baker					
57	Sebastien Grosjean	Sebastien Grosjean				
58	Thomas Johansson		Tommy Robredo			
59	Tommy Robredo	Tommy Robredo		James Blake		
60	Gustavo Kuerten					
61	James Blake	James Blake				
62	Igor Andreev		James Blake			
63	Rafael Nadal	Rafael Nadal				
64	Scoville Jenkins					

In the **knock-out draw**, top players are usually seeded and put in different parts of the draw. The ideal scenario is for the first and second seeded players to meet in the final. The names above are from the US Open of 2005; the round of 64 competitors is, in the US Open, called Round 2.

COMPETITIONS

Round robin

In a round robin, each player is placed in a group and plays against every other group member. The group winners and runners-up eventually play each other to determine the champion. This format ensures you will play a number of matches, but it will be tiring.

In the example below there are two groups of five players. The most common option would be to have the winner of group A play the runner-up of group B (and vice versa) in two semi-finals. One winner would eventually be found. A third/fourth place match could also be played. Round robins can have any number of players and groups but are ideal for small numbers who all want to play more than one match or for younger players.

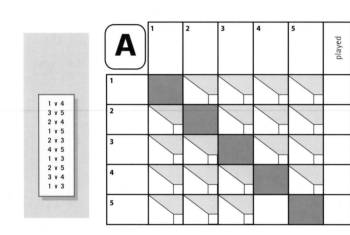

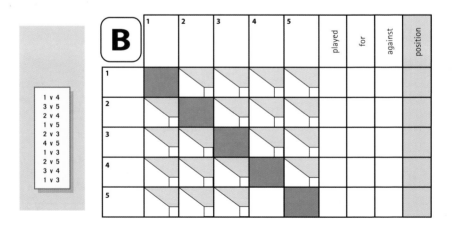

The **round robin** format is preferred when a small number of tennis players meet. They all get two or more matches before they are eliminated, depending on group size.

Knock-out with consolation

In this type of knock-out draw, players who are knocked out after their first match are entered into a "consolation" or "plate" event, guaranteeing every competitor at least two matches to play.

Two-way draw

A two-way draw is normally played with 8 to 16 players. The format starts similar to the traditional knock-out draw. If you win your first match you progress to the right of the draw. If you lose your first match you move to the left of the draw. Every player then continues to compete and plays four matches (if 16 in draw) whether they win or lose.

Progressive draw

This type of draw is ideal for club competitions because it accommodates all standards of players and gives them close matches. Knock-out draws are played in sections, with player standards determining the section he or she is in. Where possible, you play somebody of your own standard in the first match.

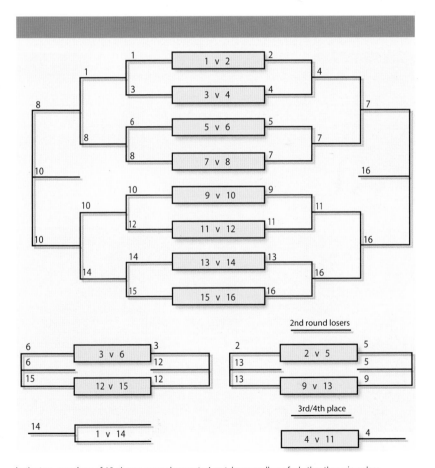

In the **two-way draw** of 16 players, every player gets 4 matches regardless of whether they win or lose.

SURFACES

Major tournaments are played on a variety of surfaces. At the highest level are the four Grand Slam events:
• Australian Open is played on rebound ace;
• French Open is played on clay;
• Wimbledon is played on grass;
• US Open is played on cement.

Each type of surface has its own playing characteristics.

Slow-paced surfaces: Clay

Clay courts vary between the red clay in Europe and the gray American clay—both have slightly different characteristics.

Clay has a rough surface, so there is more friction on the ball, which makes it bounce higher and more slowly than on other surfaces. Therefore you will have more time to reach the ball and, depending on how dry the clay is, it is possible to slide on the court surface.

You can apply more topspin to your shots when playing on clay. If you watch the experts you will see how they give the ball more height over the net, and utilize the length and width of the court to try and outmaneuver their opponent.

Rallies are longer on clay so you need to prepare yourself mentally for a long match and then use the time in between points as constructively as possible.

The best-known **clay court** tournament in the world is the French Open, which is held at Roland Garros in Paris.

Fast-paced surfaces: Grass or some indoor courts

Grass surfaces are very smooth—depending, of course, on the length of the grass and firmness of the ground. This generally means less ball friction and fast, low ball bounces. To combat the added time pressure on fast surfaces, you will need to adapt certain elements of your play, such as length of backswing and reaction speed.

The rallies are generally shorter on grass courts because the ball moves faster and so it is harder to return.

Players who use power and speed in their serves and attacking shots tend to do well on the grass courts. If you are able to dominate your games using net play, this tactic will be particularly effective.

Medium-paced surfaces: Synthetic, indoor, or hard cement courts

Medium-paced surfaces are smoother, with less ball friction than clay courts. The ball bounce is faster and medium in height, meaning a quicker pace of game than on the slow surfaces. Rallies can be of varying lengths, allowing the use of a wide variety of shots and court tactics.

You will need to use your footwork effectively on these surfaces and be mentally prepared for long or short rallies.

The US Open is played on a medium-paced, **hard-court,** cement surface.

Wimbledon is the only major tournament still played on grass courts.

> **HINT**
>
> Try to experience playing and competing on different surfaces. It is fun and will challenge your strategy and tactics.

EQUIPMENT

As a beginner, you may start by borrowing equipment from a coach or friend. However, if you start to play regularly you will need to choose your own equipment. Here are some guidelines for choosing items to suit you.

The racket

This is the most important piece of equipment you will buy, so it is worth spending a little more time and money on it to ensure you select well. There are numerous racket manufacturers and a vast range from which to choose.

Racket length

The standard length for an adult racket is 27in (68cm), although models are available as long as 29in (73cm).

If you are a young player or are buying for a child then you will need to look more carefully at the length of racket you choose. Children's rackets can range from 17in (43cm) to 26in (65cm). Your choice will depend on the size and strength of the player.

There are a variety of **lightweight** and **short rackets**, as well as junior balls, for use by younger players.

Racket weight

The weight of a 27in (68cm) racket will vary from 9oz (260g) to 12oz (340g). The weight that suits you will depend on your strength, your style of play, and your personal preference. It is a good idea to try a racket before buying it to see if the weight suits you. Many shops have demonstration rackets available for trial. Perhaps you could also experiment with rackets belonging to your club, coach, or friends to help guide the decision.

Racket grip size

As your grip is an important aspect of your technique, the grip size (circumference) of the racket handle is a key consideration when selecting a racket.

Grip sizes can vary from 4⅛in (10.25cm) to 5in (12.5cm). When trying out different sizes, look out for a grip that enables you to grasp the racket firmly and comfortably. It should be just possible for your thumb and forefinger to touch each other around the racket grip.

If your grip size is too large, you may find it difficult to keep a firm hold of the racket. If it is too small, you may have trouble altering your grip and directing the ball.

It is possible to replace the grip on your racket handle to alter the size and texture of the grip. A wide range of racket grips are available, of varying thicknesses and fabrics.

Grips can be adjusted to suit your preference. Having a clean and fresh grip certainly helps avoid any slipping of the racket in the hand.

Racket head size
You will find that rackets also vary in their head size. The area of the racket face can range from 95sq in (613sq cm) to 112sq in (722sq cm). Professional players tend to use the smaller head sizes, while club players or older players frequently opt for a larger racket face.

Racket strings
Two types of racket strings are available:
• natural gut strings—made from animal intestine;
• synthetic strings—made from materials such as polyester or titanium, or combinations of these.

Natural gut strings are much more expensive than synthetic strings, but have the advantage of greater elasticity. Rackets can be strung at a higher tension when using these strings.

Synthetic strings have evolved over the years and are perfectly adequate for club-level players. However, it is not possible to string a racket at very high tensions when using synthetic strings, because they will lose their elasticity.

Stringing and restringing rackets
When you buy a racket you may want to choose your own strings. Many sports shops offer racket stringing as a service, or you may find a stringing contact through your coach or club. Most tennis rackets will come with guidelines for suitable stringing tension levels.

It is necessary to restring your racket at intervals (or if you break a string), depending on how frequently you play. A guideline is to restring your racket as many times per year as you play tennis per week. Professionals' rackets are re-strung overnight during tournaments to maintain the preferred tension.

The balls
There is a range of tennis balls on the market, varying in quality, color, and cost.

The high-quality, more expensive balls are likely to be firmer and to last longer than cheaper ones. As you play and progress, you might prefer to play with new balls on a regular basis even though this would involve greater expense.

Although a variety of ball colors are available, club and match regulations will require that you play with yellow or white balls (although white balls are very rarely used).

If you are a beginner, you might want to practice using softer, low-compression balls.

Some **modern rackets**, such as the left- and right-hand rackets here, have a small device on the strings to prevent string vibration.

Tournament balls are sealed in pressurized cans prior to use.

CLOTHING

Choose **shoes that feel comfortable**, but also think about the surfaces you will be playing on.

Shoes

Choosing an appropriate pair of shoes in which to play tennis is almost as important as selecting the right racket. Your shoes should be light and supple, fit properly, and give you support in the right places.

Fit

As with any sports shoes, it is essential that your tennis shoes are correct for your feet. It is therefore a good idea to ask for help with fitting in the shop, because a well-fitting shoe can be surprisingly hard to judge.

It is important that your shoes give you adequate support around the ankle, because tennis involves regular and varied impact on this area.

Soles

Different styles of shoe sole are suitable for each type of court surface. Choose your shoes according to the court surface you play on most regularly:
• regular slip-proof and hard-wearing shoes are suitable for most outdoor surfaces, such as clay or tarmac;
• when playing on grass, shoes with "pimped" soles are best;
• when playing indoors, regulations may require that you wear smooth-soled shoes.

If you are playing tennis regularly, it is a good idea to have two pairs of shoes so that you can leave one to air or dry. You may also need to have more than one type of shoe if you play on more than one surface.

Clothing

Traditionally, tennis clothing is entirely white, and some clubs and tournaments will uphold this in their regulations. However, fashions change every year and some players do add color to their outfits.

Men's clothing

The basic items you will need are:
• shirt—can be collared or round necked;
• shorts—these vary in length, with longer shorts becoming increasingly popular.

When going on court, it is useful to have a **large bag** for extra rackets, grips, clothing, and refreshments.

Women's clothing
The basic items you will need are:
• shirt—can be collared or round necked;
• shorts or skirt (ideal with ball shorts);
• tennis dress—some women may choose to wear a dress in warmer weather.

Other clothing for players of both sexes
Further basic items that players will need are:
• socks—crew socks are the most effective style to wear because they support the ankles and protect them in poor weather;
• track suit—in training or in cold weather it is useful to have a track suit, but it is generally not possible to wear this on court or in competition;
• visor or cap—in sunny conditions protection for your eyes is essential.

Racket bags
It is important to protect your racket with a cover or keep it in a bag. Racket bags come in various sizes. If you have more than one racket, use a larger bag. It is possible to find a bag that will carry as many as ten rackets!

Ultimately you should aim to feel confident in your court attire. Sweat bands are an additional item possibly worth having in your racket bag.

HINT

Your racket bag is also useful for carrying extra pieces of equipment that might be needed on court, or before or after a game.
For example:
• a drinks bottle and snack;
• first-aid equipment such as band-aids for blisters;
• spare clothing items;
• a towel.

BEGINNING AND PROGRESSING

You can start learning to play tennis at **any age**...in fact, the sooner the better.

Why tennis?

Tennis is a worthwhile sport to pick up at any age, for many reasons.

Tennis is fun

It is exciting to hit that slice serve out wide and watch your opponent struggle to return it, while you run into the net and hit the volley for a winner.

Tennis is fascinating

There is a wide range of technical and tactical skills to learn, understand, and develop in the game.

Tennis offers variety

Not only can you work on your own skills and confidence but you can also have the opportunity to test these against all sorts of competitors, on different courts and in diverse environments.

Tennis is inclusive

It is a sport you can play at any age—from three or four years through to your later years. Some people still play regularly in their 80s! The game can be adapted to include players of all ages, so there are no limits on who you play the game with.

Tennis provides healthy exercise

The activity in the game works many of your larger muscle groups, of both the lower and upper body. You have to twist and turn, to run and jump, and really test your physical conditioning. Learning to play tennis provides a structure for developing your personal fitness.

Tennis is sociable

People of all ages play tennis for the social opportunities it provides. Lessons, clubs, competitions, and tennis holidays are all a great way to meet new people. This can also be an asset when traveling or moving to a new area.

Tennis is affordable

While there is a range of equipment available, once you have your racket and ball there is no need to spend a fortune on expensive clothing, further equipment, overseas travel, or accommodation to play the sport.

Taking lessons

If you want to start to play tennis as an adult one of the best ways to do so is to seek out a professional tennis coach and take a few lessons to see if you enjoy the game. Lessons can be given on an individual basis, in a pair, or in a group. If you are concerned about how capable you are, you may find an individual lesson is the best way to start the learning process.

When searching for a tennis coach you will need to ensure that they are qualified and have some form of identification. There are various tennis qualifications depending on the country you are in but most are recognized universally.

Coaches charge different amounts—a lower-level coach is likely to be less expensive than a high-level performance one. A good coach will take an active interest in you as a person, will adapt to your needs, and alter his or her teaching methods to suit you, the individual.

Coaches can be placed into one of three categories.

Development coaches

These are qualified to teach those playing tennis for the first time. They specialize in helping you improve your basic skills, to reach a level where you play the game independently.

Club coaches

These specialize in teaching confident players, helping maintain and improve technical skills and style of game. A club coach will support you in competitive tennis as far up as he or she can, encouraging and developing your match play.

Performance coaches

These will take the top players and aim to make the most of your achievements in tennis, guiding their careers and supporting ongoing training and development. Ensure you ask what qualification the coach has.

Developing a **good relationship** with a coach is very important.

DEVELOPING YOUR GAME

Different coaches—different methods

Think carefully about what motivates you, so that you can find a coach who complements you as a person.

All coaches should have a high level of technical and tactical knowledge to help you improve your game. It is valuable to work with someone who has extensive experience of tennis, to inspire you and expand your knowledge of the game. The three main coaching styles are as follows.

Authoritarian or dictatorial
Your coach will lay out plans and schedules for your development, and assess your progress within their own structure. He or she will work with little input from the player.

Democratic or cooperative
Your coach will work with you to develop a structure of learning, taking into account your preferences and adapting to your personal situation.

Laissez-faire
Your coach will adopt a more casual and fun approach, suiting players who are simply looking to enjoy the game of tennis.

Joining a club

Whether you begin getting coaching or not, if you want to play more tennis the best place to experience this is at a local club. Club sizes can range from a two-court outdoor club in a village to a larger, extensively equipped commercial one. Costs to join will depend on the facilities available.

There are many things to consider when choosing a club to join. Have a good look around and consider the following factors.

Costs
• are individual membership fees affordable;
• are there options provided for joint/family/child membership;
• which available facilities are included in the membership fee?

Modern clubs offer a range of facilities, and often have indoor courts allowing year-round guaranteed play.

Facilities
• how many courts are there? Do they get very busy;
• are the courts both indoor and outdoor;
• are outdoor courts lit for evening play;
• are there time restrictions on court use;
• are there any extra facilities, such as fitness equipment and changing rooms;
• are tennis balls provided?

Coaching
• are there a variety of contacts or options;
• can the club arrange approved, individual coaching should you require it;
• is there an option for group learning?

Competitions
• will you benefit from an opportunity to take part in competitions;
• does the club organize friendly competitions as well as internal leagues;
• do club members take part in external league competitions?

Social events
• one of the main advantages of a tennis club is the social aspect—does the club hold regular events that you can take part in?

Guests
• does the club accept guests;
• can you arrange a match against someone from another club?

Try before you buy
• is it possible to test out the facilities and meet the staff/coaches before you make the decision to join;
• does the club hold open days or publicity events that you can attend?

Once you have chosen a club, make an effort to get involved in social events and meet fellow members. You may find that you meet people in similar situations to yourself, with comparable aspirations and hesitations about playing the game of tennis.

Some large clubs in Europe are open to members and host major competitions—as here in Monte Carlo.

HINT

You will often have to commit to a fixed length of membership when joining a club, so make sure you find out as much as you can before you join.

BASIC FITNESS LEVELS

Kim Clijsters has strength and "stretch" in **perfect balance**.

You will need to decide exactly what you want from the game of tennis, but to achieve your full potential you will have to spend a great deal of time working on your fitness. The modern game of tennis requires high fitness levels—this is now an integral part of the game.

The game is demanding because the "fitness" it requires means all-round athleticism. Speed, endurance, agility, hand-eye coordination, concentration, and resistance to injury are all important.

Many top players, although possessing incredible all-round fitness, also have an extra dimension. Look, for example, at the athletic ability of Venus Williams, the strength of Andy Roddick, the power of Marat Safin, the flexibility of Maria Sharapova, the stamina of Rafael Nadal, and the speed and grace of Roger Federer. These players are highly tuned athletes who dedicate a lot of time to fitness. If you too want to reach your personal goals, you are well advised to work on all-round fitness

and try to develop your own "extra dimension." It might be this aspect that helps you to overcome your opponents.

Also, you will need to remember that tennis is an "interval" sport—there are short bursts of activity interspersed with rest periods. You should be aware of this and use it to your advantage.

Developing your own fitness
Of course, top tennis players have the time and resources to take the fitness requirements of the game to new levels. Players use the sport sciences to ensure that every detail of their physique is attended to and that their fitness programs are optimal.

To get the most out of your development as a player, you have to devote the amount of time and energy that matches your own lifestyle. However, there are "windows of opportunity" when different aspects of fitness should be worked on.

From an early age, it is important to work on the "ABCs" of athleticism:

- agility;
- balance;
- coordination.

If you are serious about your tennis you will need to get fit to play the game, rather than use tennis as a means of getting in shape. You should work on developing a fitness program to suit your individual situation. This may require the advice of your doctor and/or a fitness instructor. You should consult your doctor before starting any significant attempt to increase your levels of exercise.

Players aspiring to reach higher levels are tested in a variety of ways to see what their starting fitness levels are, carefully identifying areas that need attention. The type of fitness program you will need will be totally specific to you. Your standard of fitness will depend on:

- age and lifestyle;
- hereditary factors;
- training and starting fitness;
- diet;
- illness and injury;
- rest and recovery;
- your attitude to training and goals.

The basic principles of training

Keep these ideas in mind as you develop your training program:

- progression—move from easy to more difficult activities;
- reversibility—"if you don't use it, you lose it"—it takes a long time to get to a good fitness level but only two weeks to lose it;
- overload—in order to improve you will need to be pushed to a level beyond that which you are used to. This will mean your trainer will adjust the frequency, intensity, and duration of the exercises you use;
- variation—ensure the training is fun and varied to keep your interest and motivation levels high. Ensure you have an easy session following a hard one. You will need rest and recovery periods;
- individualism—the program you use must be individual to suit your needs;
- specificity—your program must be specific to the needs of the game of tennis. Short bursts of activity followed by rest periods reflect the pace of the game;
- remember that your fitness program should include a wide variety of exercises that will focus on different areas of skill and strength.

UNDERSTANDING FITNESS

The fitter the player, the better the performance. At the highest level the fitness of a player can make the difference between winning and losing a match. There are numerous benefits to having a good physical conditioning program—fitness delays the onset of fatigue and promotes faster recovery after competition. It will help build your confidence in match situations, knowing that you can get to every ball and that you will not tire. It will benefit your technique, make you more powerful, and reduce injuries, Above all, a good level of fitness will improve your general health and well-being and help you to enjoy your tennis.

For a serious player, the fitness program will form an essential part of his or her annual plan. Often there will be a physical training block of four to six weeks, which will then be tapered off nearer to competition. During the competitive phase, fitness will be maintained. Most top players plan the year carefully so that they can "peak" for the most important tournaments.

It is important to take your fitness seriously—consult a professional such as a physical conditioning specialist who will help you with your overall program.

WARMING UP

The warm-up

The warm-up prepares you for activity to come. The main effect is to raise your body temperature—warm muscles are more efficient than cold ones. This will help reduce the risk of injury. A good warm-up is also good mental preparation for any physical activity.

Spend 10–15 minutes warming up. Start with five minutes of jogging, skipping, or cycling followed by dynamic stretching, coordination work (younger players in particular), and some speed work.

Skipping

This is an ideal way to raise the body temperature. Skip for five minutes on the spot using a variety of skipping types:
• two feet together;
• alternating feet;
• side to side;
• forward and backward;
• hopping on right foot and then left foot;
• high knees;
• sideways jumps over a line;
• forward and backward jumps over a line.

You might also skip in circuits, changing the type of skip every 20-30 jumps.

One warm-up technique is court skipping. Start in the tramlines. Skip:
• forward to the net;
• sideways across the court;
• backwards down the tramline;
• sideways along the baseline back to the start position.

Repeat three times and vary the skipping.

Dynamic stretching

Dynamic stretching can be done across the court. You will need a variety of exercises to work the arms, shoulders, trunk, and legs:
• jog across the court circling your arms forward, then jog backward circling your arms backward;
• side skip across the court with your arms swinging across your body and then repeat moving back;
• use crossover steps moving across the court and back.

Lunges

Tennis involves many lunging movements so it is important to warm up the muscles in your groin:
• keep your back straight and your head up;
• looking forward, lift your right leg and lunge forward, ensuring the knee does not go over the toe;
• lift the left leg up and lunge forward;
• continue across the court, backwards and forwards.

This exercise involves balance, so keep your stomach muscles tight. A variation is to stretch your gluteus muscles, as follows:
• lift your right knee high and grasp it to your chest with your hands;
• move up onto your toes, balance, then lunge forward with your right leg;
• repeat with the left leg and move across the court.

A simple side stretch.

A forward lunge.

52

A typical **stretch sequence** commences with an upright stretch, first on a flat foot then on the toes followed by a lunge.

Cones

Cones are a fantastic way to practice a variety of footwork and coordination exercises, for both children and adults.

Cone drill

With younger children the cones exercises can be done in teams or as races, but ensure that the quality of the exercise is maintained and not rushed. In order to make these exercises more tennis related, carry a racket in your hand while doing the drills.

The following exercise will improve the lateral movement in your body:
• set out a series of cones (minimum of six) evenly spaced apart;
• move in and out of the cones like a snake using a lateral shuffle;
• ensure you have fast feet and always keep good posture.

There are numerous other exercises that you can do using cones. Try some of the following drills:
• run over the cones and then back again, placing one foot in between each;
• repeat with two feet in between each cone within the series of cones;
• sidestep over the cones and repeat facing the other way;
• do two-footed jumps over the cones;
• hop over the cones on the right foot and then on the left foot.

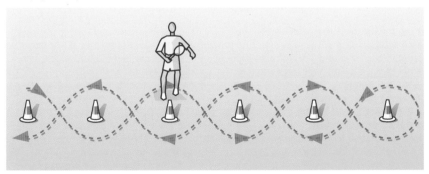

Cone drill for better lateral movement.

DRILLS

Cones and court movement

These exercises can be done with a partner. Cone drills allow you to practice more tennis-specific movement. The key here is to use the crossover step as the first step on the recovery, followed by side steps:
• position two cones on the baseline near the center mark;
• the player starts near the center mark, while the coach or partner stands on the service line with a basket of balls and throws a ball near the forehand singles sideline;

• the player moves across and hits a forehand (if right handed) down the line, then does a crossover step followed by a series of side steps back and around the front of the cone;
• the player is fed another ball and repeats this movement;
• the coach or partner then feeds a ball to near the backhand singles sideline;
• the player moves across and hits a backhand down the line, recovers around the cone, and then repeats and hits another backhand drive.

This is a simple cone run with the player **stretching down** to touch the cone at each point of the triangle. Although not always sensible, try to carry a racket for most of the speed exercises.

Ladder drills

Using a ladder is one of the best ways to work on footwork, coordination, speed, and agility and can be used by players of all ages. There are numerous exercises that you can do with a ladder. For example:
• run through the ladder with one foot in each space;
• run through it with two feet in each space;
• run through it with high knees and working the arms;
• run through it with heel flicks;
• hop through the ladder on the right foot and then on the left foot;
• jump with two feet through the ladder;
• do high jumps into every second space;
• run sideways through the ladder using side steps. Repeat, facing the other way.

Here are two ladder drill exercises, but do experiment and try some out for yourself.

Icky shuffle ladder drill
This exercise is for footwork, speed, and agility. Start this off slowly until you have the footwork pattern and then speed it up:
• place both feet to the side of the ladder;
• put your right foot into the middle and then your left foot next to it;
• move your right foot to the outside, then put your left foot into the middle of the next rung up. Follow with the right foot;
• take the left foot outside, and move the right foot to the middle of the next rung up.
Variations to this exercise are:
• to do the same drill while carrying the racket in your hand;

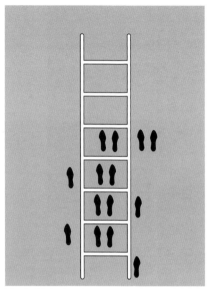

Icky shuffle ladder drill

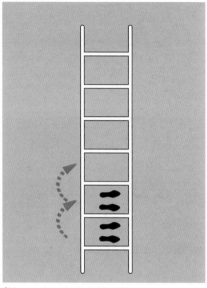

Sideways through the ladder drill

• to take a wider step outside the ladder so you can push off the outside foot more;
• to have a wider step outside the ladder and then shadow a shot each time.

Sideways through the ladder
Do this exercise carrying a racket. Always concentrate on keeping in your "ready position" throughout the drill:
• start facing sideways to the ladder and lift the leg nearest the rung up and over the rung into the next space. Bring the other foot up next to it;
• think "one, two, one, two" as you move your feet;
• ensure you do not cross your legs, and always lead with the leg nearest the rung;
• repeat, facing in the opposite direction.

Hurdles for movement
The use of hurdles for movement and plyometrics (developing speed and power) can be both fun and hard work.
   In this drill, which can be done on or off the court, blocks of three hurdles are set up with space for about three steps between each hurdle. Keep your head still, and when you sidestep across the court adopt a low ready position as you would do in the game:
• run over the hurdles and do a "split step" as you land after the third hurdle (jump slightly off the ground and then land in a wide stance);
• do a crossover step, followed by side steps to the next block of three hurdles and repeat until you have cleared all the hurdles;
• rest, then repeat three times.

HINT

Fitness is now a vital part of tennis and can be hard work, but it can also be made fun, particularly in a group environment.

DRILLS

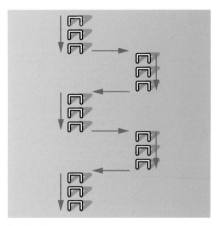

Hurdle drill

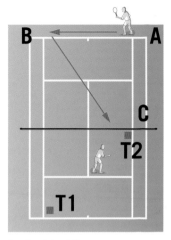

Speed training drill

All variations of this exercise can be done with a racket in your hand. For a great workout, do the following exercises for three circuits:

• put two feet in between each hurdle;
• jump over each hurdle with two feet;
• hop over each hurdle using the outside foot, so you move from your right foot onto your left foot;
• zigzag through the hurdles.

Speed training

Speed is one of the key fitness components in tennis. When doing speed work it is important you have a work-to-rest ratio of 1:5. You should rest before repeating the drill. The aim of speed work is to give 100 percent effort and get maximum speed so you will need full recovery between repetitions. Also, try to make speed training tennis-specific by ensuring the distances used are related to the game.

This fun drill is just one of many. It should be done on the court with a racket and ball, and with your coach or a partner:

• start on the tramline A on the opposite side of the court to your coach or partner, who will be positioned near the net;
• ask your coach or partner to feed a wide ball to your forehand, to B (if right handed);

• run across and hit a forehand down the line to target 1 (T1);
• ask for the next ball to be a drop shot to C;
• chase this and reply with a drop shot to target 2 (T2).

Resistance running

One of the best ways to improve your speed is to work against some resistance. In this drill your partner or coach holds a piece of elastic, which is attached to your waist. Your partner provides resistance by holding you back slightly so that you have to work harder:

• run as fast as you can over 30–50ft (10–15m), moving side to side;
• rest after each run and repeat five times.

Speed of reaction

• get your partner or coach to hold two balls, one in each hand, with his or her arms outstretched to either side;
• stand 10–13ft (3–4m) from your partner;
• get your partner or coach to drop one of the tennis balls;
• run very fast to catch the ball before it bounces twice;
• toss the ball back to your partner;
• repeat five to ten times. If you can reach the ball too easily your partner may need to move back a little.

A variation is to start with your back to your partner, then on his or her signal turn and catch the ball. You could also repeat the exercise holding your racket, trying to catch the ball on the racket strings.

Strength and power training

The medicine ball is a tremendous way to work on your strength and power. Such a ball can be used from a young age provided you use the correct weight. Children can start by using a basketball or football and then progress to a 2.2lb (1kg) medicine ball. For adults, a 4.4–8.8lb (2–4kg) ball will provide a good workout.

Here are a few throwing exercises that will work on both the upper and lower body.

Below: The value of many exercises is that they mimic parts of your tennis game. In this case a simple **sideways medicine ball throw** is similar to a forehand shot.

Overhead throws
• stand with your feet shoulder width apart;
• bring the medicine ball behind your head and then throw it as far as you can to your coach or partner. You may find it easier if you step forward with one foot as you throw the ball;
• repeat ten times.

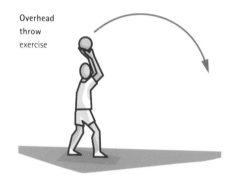

Overhead throw exercise

DRILLS

Overhead throws kneeling
• kneel on one knee, ensuring the leg is bent at a right angle;
• bring the ball from behind your head and then throw it overarm to your partner;
• repeat ten times on each knee.

Backward overhead throws
This exercise will work your arms as well as your legs:
• stand with your back to your partner holding the ball in both hands in front of your body;
• bend at your knees and then throw the ball over your head to your partner.

Forward throw
• stand with the ball in both hands in front of your body;
• bend at your knees and then throw the ball as far as you can forward.

Weight training
Dumb-bells are an easy way to start with some basic weight training and can be used at home. Begin with bells of 2.2lbs (1kg) or 4.4lbs (2kg), then increase their weight as appropriate to your strength and physique:
• hold the dumb-bells in each hand to the side of your body, then slowly raise the arms to a horizontal position (lateral raise);

Dumb-bells exercise—lateral raise

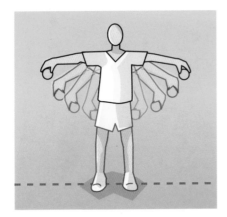

• lunge forward on your right foot, maintaining balance and posture, and keeping your back straight;
• push back and then lunge forward with your left foot;
• repeat ten times on each leg.
  Another dumb-bell exercise is to:
• hold the dumb-bells in each hand and stand erect with feet shoulder-width apart;
• raise the right hand up and above your head with a pumping action, and then do so with your left hand (don't lock your elbows);
• repeat ten times with each hand.

Plyometrics
Plyometrics involves the lengthening of the muscle group, followed by an immediate contraction, over a short period of time. This causes a forceful movement and is one of the best ways to develop more power. Skipping is a basic form of plyometrics and double-jump skipping is an excellent way to train, as is the hexagon drill:
• stand outside a marked hexagon;
• jump with two feet in and out each side as fast as you can;
• repeat three times in a row, and time how long this takes you.
  Another simple plyometric exercise is:
• position a cone about 30ft (10m) away from a sturdy box;
• start by standing on the box about 1ft (0.3m) high;
• at the command of your coach, jump from the box and do a fast sprint to the cone;
• repeat five times, and then rest.

Core stability
It is important to strengthen your abdominal area, because core stability is essential to a tennis player. The "Swiss ball" or stability ball is an excellent tool for this:
• sit on the ball with your back straight and knees and feet together;
• hold your stomach muscles in;
• lift one leg slowly 4in (10cm) off the floor and hold for 10–20 seconds, then lower it;
• repeat with the other leg;
• complete three to five lifts with each leg.

Training should be fun. Although it is important to work players hard, at every level, you should never lose sight of the fact that tennis is a great "game" and should be enjoyed. Even if you lose a match you have still gained from the exercise and recreation.

Physical training also helps with your psychological approach to the game; a fit body frees up the mind to allow you to concentrate on skills, techniques, and tactics. The old adage—applied to many sports—is still true: A bad day on the court is better than a good day in the office!

US star **Andy Roddick** enjoys his toning work on a beach in Miami.

HINT

These exercises and drills are a small sample of what can be included in an overall fitness program. Each one of these drills can be adapted and made harder or easier.

INTRODUCTION AND GRIP

The forehand is a crucial match- and point-winning shot. Although the forehand is probably the most fundamental shot in tennis, and the one you learn first, it is not necessarily simple. Advances in technology and the use of lighter rackets have enabled players to add detail to the shot such as topspin and more accurate direction. You need only look at the forehand shots of top players such as Roger Federer and Maria Sharapova to see how powerful and effective this shot has become.

You are well advised to try different grips (pages 60–63) and then match your play to the grip that suits you best (pages 64–69). If you have a coach he or she will assist you.

Andre Agassi uses an **aggressive forehand** to return a serve.

With the **eastern grip**, the hand position is behind the racket handle.

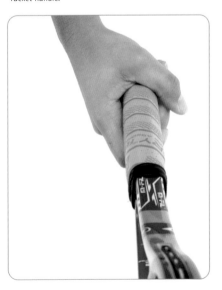

The grip

As with all the shots in tennis, there are a variety of ways to play a forehand. The main differences lie in the grip you use.

The eastern grip

This grip—also known as the shake-hands grip—is the most common at club-level tennis and is often an ideal starting point. With it, you will tend to hit flat or with slight topspin.

You can use the eastern grip with any forehand stance, semi-closed to fully open. For this grip, the palm of your hand is placed on the side of the handle, as if you are shaking hands with the racket. The contact point should be lower and farther from the body than with the semi-western or western grip. One advantage of the eastern grip is that it is easier to adapt strokes to net play than with the more extreme grips. The drawback, though, is that you may lose efficiency on clay surfaces because of reduced topspin on the ball.

The semi-western grip
This grip is the one that most top players will use most of the time. It allows for a great variety of shots to be played and increases the ability to put spin on the ball.

With the semi-western grip, the hand should be held slightly farther round the racket handle, with the palm starting to come underneath the racket. This positioning enables maximum transfer of force and spin into the shot. It also enables you to lay back your wrist while playing a forehand, giving more flexibility to the movement of the racket face.

You would normally play with a semi-open or open stance when using the semi-western grip. The contact point should be higher (approaching shoulder height) and closer to your body; it should also be more frontal (in front of your body) than for the eastern forehand.

The main disadvantage of this grip is that you may find it hard to deal with low-bouncing balls, and that you will need to alter your grip when playing at the net.

With the **semi-western grip**, the hand is farther around the handle.

BASIC STANCE

Diverse grips suit different players and are also adapted to match your stance.

The stance can vary from fully open to square and then to closed.

open stance

square stance

INTRODUCTION AND GRIP

The western grip

This grip should be held even farther around, with the hand below the handle. The western grip allows a wide "throwing action," facilitating topspin, and is used by pure baseline players and clay court specialists. It will lead to an even more pronounced laying back of your wrist and more closed racket face during the swing than with the semi-western grip. Your contact point should be even higher, closer to your body, and farther in front than the semi-western grip.

The western grip is not recommended for young players in today's game, because it has several disadvantages:

• you may have difficulty with low balls as well as fast and wide balls—making this grip more suitable for slower surfaces;

• it is harder to adapt to volleying grips;

• with such an extreme grip you would tend to have a backward thrust and therefore it may be difficult to transfer your weight forward in any shot;

• young players are more vulnerable to wrist injury with extreme grips.

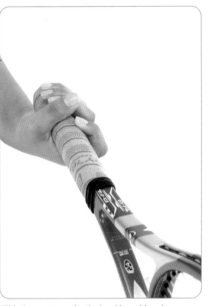

With the **western grip**, the hand is positioned even farther around the handle.

GRIP AND SHOT

In the pages concerning your choice of grip you will notice that different shots are recommended for different grips. Initially it is a good idea to find a grip that is comfortable, then slowly try to perfect different grips for each of your shots.

In a match situation you will soon find that you are changing your grip automatically, without thinking about it.

Adapting a good ready position with both hands on the racket makes it easier to **change grip**.

The two-handed grip
You may find you prefer to use two hands on the forehand.

Place your dominant hand at the bottom of the handle with an eastern or semi-western forehand grip. If you use this grip you need to be extremely quick to make up for lack of reach.

A classic **two-handed grip**.

The **two-handed grip** for a left-handed player.

The continental grip
It is difficult to deal with high-bouncing balls with this grip, which is also known as the chopper grip. Most players will use this grip for serving, volleying, and smashing and also touch shots (drop shots). If you use the continental grip you tend to play the ball "later," and it is more difficult to achieve as much power as with the semi-western grip. You may, however, use the continental grip for a sliced forehand or for a blocked return of serve. (Also see p. 88.)

The **continental grip** is rarely used for standard forehand shots but it does have some special uses.

The **continental** grip.

HINT

Try to master the semi-western grip. It is most effective for power and spin—to take the ball early and on the rise. Be modern!

PLAYING THE FOREHAND

Using the eastern forehand

The eastern forehand is most popular in club and recreational tennis. However, there are some advantages to this style. If you use the eastern forehand grip, you will tend to hold the racket more upright; this makes it easier to have a loop to the take back.

Preparation and backswing
• start in the ready position;
• as with the semi-western forehand (page 66), take the racket back in a slight loop with the aid of the non-hitting hand. This will help shoulder and trunk rotation. The non-racket arm should then act as part of the counterbalance to the movement of the racket arm throughout the action. Although the path of the racket in the backswing may vary, its purpose is really to initiate momentum for the forward swing.

Forward swing and contact point
The backswing and forward swing need to be continuous in a back-to-front action or a basic low-to-high swing:
• initially, as you prepare for the shot, your weight is on your back foot and then it is transferred onto your front foot to help generate power;
• with the eastern grip you are more likely to step down the court in a semi-closed or "square" stance;
• if using the square stance, ensure that you step with one foot in front of the other—the front and back legs should be perpendicular to the net. This stance is good for balance and for hitting a controlled shot. It will also help young players achieve good weight transfer;
• ball contact point should occur at the side and over the front foot.

The **eastern grip** forehand, backswing...

...contact point, and follow through.

64

Follow through
• after impact the racket head will move in the direction of the ball and the follow through will pass across the body (and allow recovery for the next shot);
• with the modern forehand, the follow through is more varied—as we will see in the semi-western forehand. There will also be

differences between men and women as well as variations according to the style of play and the type of shot you are going for;
• a good follow through will allow you to continue the racket head acceleration through impact—reducing the possibility of injury—and to be balanced after impact and so ready for the next shot.

If you use the eastern grip and step down the court, there will tend to be more **linear momentum** than angular momentum.

Russian Svetlana Kuznetsova attacks the ball with her forehand. Her **momentum** can take her forward if she wishes to move to the net.

> **HINT**
>
> Try to avoid a "closed" stance, where your front foot steps across your back foot, because this will restrict rotation of the trunk and hips.

THE STANCE AND THE SHOT

Jennifer Capriati plays her **one-handed forehand** from the baseline.

• ensure that you are in a position in which you are alert and ready to sprint to the ball as quickly as possible. Your stance should also be comfortable and quick to return to in between hits.

Backswing
The path of the backswing will vary with different players, but almost all modern players will use a looped preparation. This allows for a more fluent swing and also for the racket head to accelerate over a greater distance before it reaches the ball:
• as the ball is hit by your opponent, pivot the foot that is closest to the ball outwards;
• lift your elbow and begin to turn your shoulders simultaneously;
• use your non-hitting hand to guide the racket back, so the racket face is slightly closed. This will aid rotation of the shoulders;

Using the semi-western forehand
As we have seen, the modern forehand is most commonly played with the semi-western grip by professionals.

Preparation
• start from an athletic stance or the "ready position";
• position your feet shoulder width apart;
• bend your knees slightly and flex your waist marginally;
• hold the racket in front of you with two hands. Your shoulders should remain parallel to the net;

With the semi-western forehand, you should be comfortable but alert in your **ready position**.

• use the non-hitting arm to act as a counterbalance to the movement of the racket arm throughout the action.

Forward swing
• as you start the forward swing, drop your racket head and extend your bent knees to facilitate the upward movement in your shot;
• with the semi-western grip, keep your elbow close to your body in the early stages of the forward swing to ensure the stroke's stability;
• accelerate your elbow movement prior to making contact with the ball;

• rotate your trunk and keep it flexible;
• keep your head still to maintain balance throughout the stroke;
• extend your elbow in the early stages of the forward swing to "flatten out" the forehand stroke;
• with the semi-western grip, keep your racket face closed during the forward swing until the contact position;
• ensure the path of your racket in the forward swing is from low to high;
• increase your racket trajectory just before you make contact with the ball.

The **backswing** initiates momentum for the forward swing. It is guided by the movement of the elbow.

THE STANCE AND THE SHOT

Contact point
• keep your balance throughout the shot, with your head still and your eyes focussed on the hitting area;
• make contact in the open stance;
• extend your knees and turn the right hip so that your weight is transferred along the racket head trajectory of the swing both prior to and on contact;
• allow your racket head to be slightly below your wrist on contact;
• ensure you hit the ball to the side and in front of your body;
• try and have a firm grip on contact so the racket does not rotate in your hand;
• with the semi-western grip, you can lay the wrist back on contact.

Follow through
• always extend through the ball on the follow through so that you continue the acceleration of the racket through contact. If you anticipate the racket stopping, you will decrease the speed of your shot;
• watch top players because the path of the follow through is very individualistic. It will depend on your style and the shot you play, the grip you use, and also on your tactical intention. If you use a semi-western grip, your follow through will tend to be up and around your neck or higher. If you use a western grip, your follow through is likely to be shorter and lower.

The **semi-western** forward swing...

...at contact...

...and with follow through.

Using the western forehand

If you adopt the western forehand grip then you will tend to have a steep racket head trajectory, and the racket head speed is very fast on contact. You can still play the shot from an open stance, however.

Your contact point should be higher and closer to your body than for the semi-western grip. With a western grip, your forearm and wrist action should be more exaggerated and the follow through more pronounced, often being shorter and lower.

Although few players use the **western forehand**, you must choose the style that is best for you. Here the shot is shown at contact...

...and with follow through.

Leyton Hewitt hits with an **open stance** and has a follow through that does not take him forward in the shot.

HINT

A good follow through will reduce the possibility of injury by allowing normal deceleration of the racket.

LEARN FROM THE EXPERTS

One of the best ways to improve your shots is to watch and learn from professionals. When watching top players execute the forehand, try to break down the shot into separate parts and note how each part serves a purpose.

As we have described on the previous pages, there is no one ideal technique for the forehand but there is an "optimum" technique for each individual player. You will need to find yours.

Roger Federer is here preparing to play a **forehand drive**.

Open stance Notice how many top players play their forehand with an open stance. They set up with their feet virtually facing the net.

Non-hitting arm Notice how the non-hitting arm is used to assist in trunk and shoulder rotation. When the racket is taken back, observe how the shoulders are turned away from the court more than the hips, thus creating an angle of separation. This enables the forward swing to store energy and be more power generated.

Height of the take back This will vary with different players. Leyton Hewitt, for example, has a larger take back than others players. If your take back is too large, however, the chances are you will be late on the ball, unless you have Hewitt's timing!

Semi-western grip Most top players (including Roger Federer and Kim Clijsters) use the semi-western grip. This enables the wrist to be laid back more and will enable the racket to travel over a greater distance to generate more power. When you try to lay the racket head back, be careful that you do not end up slapping at the ball!

LEARN FROM THE EXPERTS

Belgian Justine Henin-Hardenne at contact on an **attacking** forehand.

Swing path Players will vary how they take the racket back. Some do a simple unit turn, some have a shallow loop, while others perform a down-to-up swing—don't confuse style with function.

Head and eyes Notice how still the head is at contact and how focussed the eyes are. The head is the heaviest part of your body and needs to be still for you to maintain balance. Head movement is a common fault with young players and results in lack of ball control.

Follow through This will vary depending on your style of play, the shot you are executing, and the grip you use, but in all cases the elbow will end up high and pointing in the direction the ball is going. Women players may have a longer follow through over the shoulder because they do not have the power of the men. With male players the racket may finish more in front of the body particularly when the player is trying to hit with excessive topspin.

Use of the legs Notice the position of the legs in the preparation, and then the back leg drive.

HINT

Watch live or recorded tennis as much as possible and observe the variations between players. The difference between males and females is due to their diverse strengths and physiques.

INTRODUCTION AND GRIP

The backhand can be played with one or two hands. In the modern game, many of the top female players use both hands. In the men's game there are more single-handed backhand players.

Both the one-handed and the two-handed shots have their advantages. For example, the one-handed backhand can provide much greater reach, which is beneficial in a fast-moving game. However, the two-handed player can achieve greater power with the extra hand. The advantage of using one or two hands will depend on your personal strengths and the style of game you are playing.

One of the main tactics to adopt is variation of spin, and this can be enhanced by the grip you choose.

The grip
As with the forehand, the way you play a backhand depends on the grip you use.

The eastern backhand grip
This grip is the easiest one to use if you choose a one-handed backhand. For the eastern backhand grip, the knuckle of your first finger should be on top of your racket, thereby ensuring that the racket face is vertical at contact point. As you progress, you should aim for more topspin in your shot. This will involve a more extreme grip, turning your hand farther round.

Many top players use this extreme grip, especially when playing on clay surfaces. It is easier to hit a high-bouncing ball, take the ball on the rise, and impart topspin onto the ball. The main disadvantage of this grip is when playing lower balls and returning hard serves on a fast surface.

The continental backhand grip
As you may have noted in the forehand section, the continental grip is mainly used for serving, volleying, and smashing. It is difficult to execute topspin with this grip, which is a major limitation when playing a backhand. However, the continental grip does have advantages when playing a slice

Roger Federer is a **one-handed backhand** exponent.

With the **eastern grip**, the knuckle of the first finger is on top of the racket.

shot. If you use this grip to hit a flat or topspin backhand you will need to have a strong wrist and excellent timing.

The simplest solution for beginners is to add the second hand to the forehand grip, thereby using **two forehand grips** to hold the racket.

Use a **continental grip** for the lower hand and an eastern forehand or semi-western forehand for the upper hand.

Use an **eastern backhand grip** for the lower hand and an eastern forehand for the upper hand.

Use an **eastern backhand** for the lower hand on the racket and an eastern forehand or semi-western forehand for the upper hand.

The two-handed backhand grip
Two-handed backhands are popular and are valuable shots to possess in your tennis repertoire. There are a variety of ways to combine grips for a two-handed backhand.

It is generally recommended that a right-handed player use a continental grip with the right hand and an eastern forehand or semi-western grip with the left hand. This will allow greater flexibility and variety with shots, and will make it easier to adjust for a one-handed slice shot.

A two-handed grip is quite individual to the player. Men tend to have the lower hand slightly farther round toward the eastern backhand than the women do, especially if playing on slow clay surfaces. They have more strength in the wrists, so it is more straightforward to hit with topspin.

Using the one-handed backhand

A strong backhand will increase power and consistency while rallying, enabling you to pass down the line and to create severe cross-court angles to challenge your opponent. The backhand may seem like a tricky shot to a beginner, but it can be learned relatively easily and, with practice, improved quite quickly. In the more advanced game the topspin backhand has become an important weapon.

As with all shots in tennis, before you develop your tactics it is important to master the fundamentals of the shot. You will be well advised to walk before you can run with this particular shot.

Your **shoulders should rotate** as you take the racket back in a one-handed backhand. You can use your left hand on the racket as a support in the take back.

Left: Justine Henin-Hardenne plays a **one-handed backhand** as a return of serve. Note the extreme grip she has used here.

Preparation and backswing
• start from your "athletic position" or ready stance;
• as soon as you see the ball is coming to your backhand, change your grip accordingly—as you take your racket back. If you are in the early stages of perfecting your backhand, use the eastern backhand grip. If you are proficient with the backhand and wanting more topspin, then use a more extreme backhand grip;
• as you take the racket back (using your non-racket hand), rotate your shoulders. This should be a single "unit" motion;
• move your racket to approximately shoulder height before you take your shot.

There are two ways to get the racket back in this position:
• turn your shoulder, take the hand back, then lift the racket to shoulder height; or
• turn the shoulder and immediately lift the hand into position, then have a loop to your take back. For the beginner a simple unit turn with slight loop is the simplest.

HINT

There is a temptation to "run around" a backhand to make it a forehand shot. Try to avoid this (although it can be a useful skill) and make your backhand as strong a shot as your forehand.

ONE-HANDED BACKHAND

The **one-handed** swing...

...at contact...

Forward swing and contact point
• make the backswing and forward swing in a continuous action in order to increase the racket head speed;
• having taken the racket back, step down the court with your right foot (if right handed) toward the ball, in order to play the shot in a square stance;

• as you start the forward swing, the head of the racket will drop below the height of the oncoming tennis ball;
• bend your knees to help you lift the path of the racket to the height of the ball;
• the contact point should be to the side and in front of your body. At impact, hit the ball in front of the front foot;
• usually extend your elbow joint so your arm is almost straight on impact, thus increasing racket-head speed.

...and with follow through.

Follow through
• move the path of the racket head from low down to high up;
• as you hit through the ball, bring your racket upward;
• finish with your racket well out in front of your body, with the racket head poised above your wrist;
• use your non-racket hand as a counterbalance, it will move slightly behind you;
• bring your back foot round after the initial part of the follow through, in order for your racket and body to decelerate slowly.

The **single-handed backhand** is mostly played with a square stance.

You should avoid "**closing**" your stance by stepping across the tennis court—this will restrict your follow through.

Some top players hit a single-handed backhand from an open stance, but this requires a great deal of strength in the trunk and wrist. It is considerably easier to achieve effective weight transfer by stepping forward and into the shot.

Kim Clijsters executes a tremendously **powerful backhand**. Despite the energy that goes into this shot her head remains still and her eyes focussed.

HINT

Always keep your head still and over the ball, aiming to maintain balance as you strike the ball.

TWO-HANDED BACKHAND

Frenchman Arnaud Clement looks well positioned and comfortable with his **two-handed backhand**.

Using the two-handed backhand

The two-handed backhand explosion really came about with US star Chris Evert in the 1970s. Once she had won Wimbledon, she was a great role model for this shot. To quote her father, Jimmy Evert: "I didn't teach the two-hander to her. She started that way because she was too small and weak to swing the backhand with one hand. I hoped she'd change—but how can I argue with this success?" The key point was that she felt "too small and weak" to manage a single-handed shot. The two-hander certainly provides the possibility of more power.

The great role models in the men's game were Jimmy Connors and Bjorn Borg. When he won Wimbledon—five times—Borg dispelled the myth that a two-handed player could not win on fast surfaces such as grass!

The two-handed backhand has many advantages for a player:
- it is easier for young players because two hands provide more strength;
- you have to place the other hand on the racket only in the initial stages, without worrying about grips;
- it is easier to hit the higher-bouncing balls with aggression;
- you can get more disguise than with the one-handed backhand because of a slightly later contact with the ball.

Preparation
• start from your "athletic" position or ready stance, and keep mentally alert;
• as soon as you see the ball coming to your backhand side, adjust your grip. Don't forget grips will vary with different players;
• initially, keep the take back simple, with a shallow loop. The degree of loop is an individual preference. Some players take the racket straight back, while others move the racket back high, and yet others low;
• the distance your arms are from your body on the take back will vary with different players. Young players tend to have their arms closer to their bodies. As they get stronger (especially the men) their arms straighten more on the take back and the contact point is therefore farther away.

Ready stance...

...take back for the two-handed backhand...

...shoulder turn...

TWO-HANDED BACKHAND

Forward swing and contact point
• having turned at the shoulders and taken the racket back, step forwards to transfer your weight into the shot. This is your square stance;
• use your footwork and movement patterns to allow you to maintain balance and be in the correct position to hit the ball;

• move the racket forward in a low-to-high swing of the racket head;
• ensure your contact point is to the side and in front of the front foot—the distance will vary, depending on the grips you use;
• position the racket face so it is vertical to the ground on contact with the ball.

...forward swing...

...contact point...

Follow through
• hit through the ball and follow through up and over your shoulder, allowing recovery for movement to the next shot;
• as you hit through the ball, try and extend your arms forward, so that the elbows are lifted up and the racket can then finish over your shoulder.

...and follow through.

CHECK YOUR STANCE

Many two-handed backhands are now played with an open stance (above). This usually occurs when returning a wider ball, when the player is trying to hold his or her ground on the baseline and not be taken off the court. It is also used frequently on the return of a hard first serve.

You need to be quite strong to control the ball with an open stance. For young or novice players, it is best to stick to a square stance (above) when making your shot. This will generate more power by transferring body weight into the shot.

Belgian Xavier Malisse watches the result of his **two-handed backhand**. He keeps his head still, his eyes on the ball, and his hands (for this particular shot) a little distance apart.

HINT

On your follow through, extend through the ball and lift the elbows high so that they are pointing down the court.

LEARN FROM THE EXPERTS

Roger Federer has one of the best one-handed backhands in world tennis, and he is an excellent role model for this shot.

Here Federer is in the optimum hitting zone on his backhand side—meaning that he is at an ideal distance from the ball. In order for your backhand to be consistent, so you can make repeated strokes without errors, you will need to hit the ball consistently in this zone. Here Federer has positioned himself a comfortable distance from the ball so that he can freely execute the shot.

Roger Federer gets down low to play his **one-handed backhand.**

Steady head Federer's head is still and over the ball with his eyes clearly focussed on the ball. This helps to maintain excellent balance as he plays the shot.

Weight transfer As Federer steps down the court he moves his weight forward.

Arm angle The arm is virtually straight when he is about to hit the ball and his grip is firm.

Leg position As Federer gets down to the ball, he is bending at the knees as well as the waist. Notice the definition in the right calf muscle, which is evidence of the great lower body strength he has gained.

Swing path The racket head is slightly below the height of the ball because the swing path is in an upward direction, so Federer can impart topspin onto the ball.

Extreme grip Federer uses an extreme backhand grip— this will enable him to hit with more topspin.

Front foot Federer's right foot is planted flat onto the ground as he moves his weight forward and onto it.

Back foot The left heel is coming off the ground, showing that Federer has transferred his weight forward into the shot.

HINT

Focus on finding your optimum hitting zone and then consistently hit the ball in that area.

LEARN FROM THE EXPERTS

There are slight differences between the top female and top male players on the two-handed backhand. These are mainly due to differences in physique and strength.

These two photos reveal minor differences—notably how straight the arms are—but there are also many similarities in technique.

Serena Williams puts everything into her backhand return.

Serena Williams

Here we can see how Serena Williams is playing this backhand from an open stance, thereby revealing her tremendous strength. She has lined her back (left) leg up close to the flight of the ball with her front leg farther away. Use of the open stance will help Williams to recover quicker and save her half a step. Also notice how much upper body rotation she achieves with her shoulder turn. On contact the racket head was close to her body and below the height of the ball. As the shot was played, Williams also straightened her wrists as the last stage in the coordination chain (see page 89). This provides her with greater pace on the ball.

Although her weight started on the back foot, it is ready to be transferred forward and into the shot.

Andre Agassi watches his **two-handed** return.

Andre Agassi

This top player boasts one of the most economical and effective backhands in the game. His routine is to have a simple take back with a slight loop to the swing.

Ideally Andre Agassi likes to prepare early, taking the racket up slightly. He also has good shoulder rotation—the shoulder rotation is used to take the racket back and his weight is on the back foot. He uses a wide, stable stance. From this position Agassi can either play the shot from a semi-open stance or step down the court in more of a square stance—in both cases transferring his weight into the shot.

The main difference on the take back between Agassi and Serena Williams is how close their arms and rackets are to their bodies. Because men have greater strength in their arms and wrists, they tend to straighten their arms more than women and as a result will make contact with the ball slightly farther away from the body.

The distance Agassi's arms are from his body will ensure he can then make contact with the ball in a comfortable hitting zone. His arms are fully extended, having driven the racket forward to make contact. The racket head is raised slightly at the back, creating a longer lever for added speed on the ball.

In the photograph you can see that Agassi has good upper body rotation but his head is still facing the ball and is still. His eyes are focussed on the ball.

> **HINT**
>
> Whatever your style of take back, ensure you master good shoulder rotation and early preparation.

INTRODUCTION AND GRIP

The serve is the most important shot in the game of tennis. It is the starting point of every game, and the first opportunity to dominate the point being played. If you can hold your serve consistently, you can defend your game right up to a tie-break. While the serve can be your winning strength it can also be a liability.

The keys to a good serve are a combination of consistency, accuracy, variety, power, and disguise. Although there is no single technique and players will develop their own style, there are certain important factors that form the basis of the serve sequence:

• preparation—you will need a good starting stance or ready position;
• grip—you will need a confident and reliable grip of the racket;
• power—you will need an effective and powerful "loading position";
• contact point—you will need a solid and consistent point of contact with the ball;
• follow through.

THE GRIP

As a beginner you may want to start with the eastern forehand, or shake-hands, grip. This is relatively easy to master and will give a confident hold of the racket and enable you to get the ball into court.

The more advanced and optimum grip for the serve is known as the continental, or chopper, grip. This grip will enable you to hit with greater controlled power and to impart spin more easily. (Also see page 63.)

The **eastern grip** is the most common grip for the forehand shot. When beginning the serve you can use this grip.

The **continental grip** is ideal for the serve. Hold the racket as if chopping wood; the "V" of the thumb and forefinger is slightly to the left of the shaft.

Once you have mastered the basic throwing action, try to develop your own serve by progressing to the continental grip. It may be difficult to break the habit of the simple eastern forehand grip, but it is a necessary step in order to achieve a competitive serve and one that you can develop satisfactorily.

The success of many top players, such as **John McEnroe** (left), Pete Sampras, Roger Federer, Venus Williams, and Maria Sharapova has been largely due to the power and effectiveness of their serves.

Wrist
Elbow
Arm
Shoulder
Trunk
Hips
Legs

The serve should **gain momentum** as force is transferred up through the body.

The coordination chain

Although individuals may vary, central to every player's serve is the principle known as the body's "coordination chain." This is the passage of power through the body and into the shot. There are many movements within a serve during which the body acts as a chain of links, transferring the force generated in one body part to the next in the chain.

For an optimum technique, the coordination chain must occur in the correct sequence; through the legs, hips, trunk, shoulder, arm, elbow, then wrist. This will enhance power and control, delay fatigue, and help prevent injury.

HINT

You can develop your own variations on the continental grip. Gripping slightly farther to the backhand side can aid spin techniques. If you have a strong wrist, a grip more to the forehand will help with power.

THE STANCE

Serving with power

In order to make the serve effective, there are some fundamentals in technique that must to be adhered to. Let's look at the key features of a powerful serve.

A **steady and consistent set-up** aids serving, so don't be rushed. Play each serve with full concentration.

Preparation
- always start with the correct stance, so you are balanced for your throwing action;
- adopt a comfortable, sideways stance;
- position your feet roughly shoulder width apart behind the baseline, with the front foot pointing slightly towards the net and the back foot parallel with the baseline;
- your weight can be on the back foot (see Sharapova, above) or on your front foot;
- initially, hold the ball and racket together, pointing toward the targeted service box;

- for a beginner the movement of the racket and ball placement arms should be synchronized so there is a smooth rhythm to the serve;
- keep your weight on your back foot as you begin the ball placement;
- hold the ball with your fingertips, with the palm of the hand facing upward. Release it from a straight arm at about shoulder height;
- as your arm moves upwards, the weight of your body should start to shift forward. Some players will have a slight circular motion to their ball toss, whereas others use a straight vertical toss.

...start of ball toss...

Preparation...

...ball toss...

...loading position with the left arm higher than the right arm...

Throwing action
• as your legs thrust upward, your racket will fall down your back, before the throw forward begins;
• the farther down your back the racket is allowed to fall, the more power you can generate in your throwing action.

Ball toss
• if you are a beginner, toss the ball slightly forward and to the right (toward your expected contact point). As you become more confident, this may vary;
• aim to toss the ball higher than the reach of your arm, because usually the ball is hit when it has just begun to fall;
• ensure your racket take back is continuous, and the racket face remains perpendicular (closed) to the ground as you get into the loading position.

Many players will develop **small rituals**—such as how they hold the ball and racket—to help their concentration.

THE DELIVERY

There are two basic types of footwork used in the serve. Both can be highly effective—you will need to find the one that suits you.

Foot up
With foot-up, or platform, style, the player brings his or her back foot up directly behind the front foot when reaching for the ball, enabling a tall upward stretch. He or she then falls onto the front foot after the drive. This action produces great vertical force and a high contact position for the player.

Foot back
Here the player leaves his or her back foot behind, bending deeply at the knees. After the drive, the landing is on the front foot. Larger horizontal forces are produced using this technique.

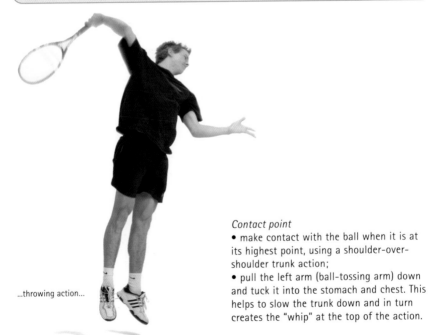

...throwing action...

Contact point
• make contact with the ball when it is at its highest point, using a shoulder-over-shoulder trunk action;
• pull the left arm (ball-tossing arm) down and tuck it into the stomach and chest. This helps to slow the trunk down and in turn creates the "whip" at the top of the action.

...contact point...

...and follow through.

- you should land inside the court on your front foot;
- the kick back of the other leg is the reaction force needed to ensure you are dynamically balanced;
- as your serve develops, your follow through may become shorter with a strong elbow bend, but this position is not recommended for beginners.

Follow through
- after making contact with the ball, continue the internal rotation of the upper arm and pronation of your forearm;
- ensure the path of the racket is toward the racket side of the body before it moves across to the opposite side of the body, to allow you to move forward into the court;

HINT

Everybody has their own style, but the great servers all have good rhythm. Focus on achieving a reliable and comfortable rhythm in your own serve.

SERVE VARIATIONS

Russian Marat Safin is a great exponent of the **topspin serve**.

The reality is that advanced players will rarely hit a straight, flat serve. Mostly, the ball will have some degree of spin on it. The two basic variations on the serve are the topspin and the slice.

The topspin serve
This type of serve will give you a wider margin for error than a flat serve. It crosses higher over the net before the spin brings the ball down, causing it to bounce higher after hitting the ground. The rougher the surface, the higher the ball will bounce, so this shot is particularly effective when used on clay.

The topspin serve is used more in the men's game than the women's. Women do not have the same physical strength as the men to achieve excessive topspin on the ball—and if the topspin serve is not effective your opponent will easily control the point.

The **topspin serve** stance...

Preparation
• your stance should be the same as for the flat serve (page 90).

94

The ball's **trajectory** in a well-executed topspin serve (B) is much higher than in a flat serve (A).

...and follow through.

Follow through
• direct the first part of your follow through outwards from your body, and to your right;
• some players even finish with their racket arm passing by their right leg.

...contact point...

...loading position...

Contact point
• the swing of your racket head to contact the ball should be from behind and to the left of your head;
• move your racket from left to right—upwards, across, and over the ball (for a right-handed player).

Loading position
• toss the ball slightly behind the head, over your left shoulder (for a right-handed player);
• lean the upper body backwards a little and ensure that there is a good knee bend.

SERVE VARIATIONS

Slice serve expert Marat Safin.

The slice serve stance...

The slice serve

This type of serve forces your opponent to move out of the court area in order to return the ball, because the spin takes the ball to the side.

The slice serve is very effective on fairly smooth surfaces, such as indoor courts and grass, where the impact of the sidespin is more pronounced.

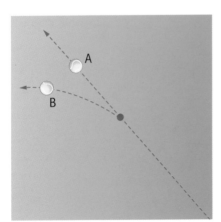

Preparation
• your stance should be the same as for your flat serve (page 90).

With the slice serve, the ball's **trajectory** has a leftward curl (to point B), whereas after the flat serve it would travel in a straight line (to point A).

The slice serve can be effective in moving your opponent to beyond the court lines, as well as in swinging the ball into the body of your opponent, and so "jamming" him or her to force a weak return. The slice serve is not only used as a first serve, but also often as a second serve in the women's game.

...loading position...

...contact point...

... and follow through.

Loading position
• toss the ball in front of your body and slightly to your right (for a right-handed player);
• turn the upper body slightly sideways and backwards, to get good shoulder rotation.

Contact point
• ensure your contact with the ball is in a sideways motion, across the ball. This will inflict the sideways spin on the ball;
• your contact point should be farther to the right than with your flat serve.

Follow through
• allow your upper body to follow the path of the ball in the direction of the shot.

HINT

Once you have mastered the topspin and slice serves, work on disguise. Can you hit either flat, topspin, or slice from the same ball toss?

Pete Sampras is renowned for the power of his serve. Although he has incredible reliability, power, and disguise in his serve, the platform of his success lies in his excellent loading position—or optimal throwing position. This is the basis of his coordination chain.

The degree of knee bend in the loading position will be individual to every player, but Sampras' great strength allows him a deep knee bend. This enables him to push "into" the ground, using it as a springboard to propel his throw. Power comes from the ground in the form of ground reaction force. The knee bend and push (flexion and extension) have to be coordinated. (This is often difficult in young players and should not be introduced too early.)

Body position The angle of the body is key to a good loading position, because the leading arm follows the ball toss and "pulls" the serving arm up after it.

Left arm Notice how straight the arm is on the ball toss. This is essential in achieving an accurate ball placement. It also helps to "pull" him up to the ball.

Left elbow This is held away from the body and the shoulders are aligned diagonally, so that the left shoulder is higher than the right. This provides the optimum throwing position. The racket face is closed.

Rotation Sampras' hip rotation and trunk rotation are the next stages after legs in the serve coordination chain.

Knee bend This facilitates extra spring in the serve.

Left: One of the keys to Pete Sampras' consistent serves is his excellent **loading position.** In this stance he has good knee flexion and rotation of the hips and shoulders. Sampras uses the foot-back technique, so his back foot remains behind the front one until the shot is played.

HINT

A good strong loading position can often be found by staggering the arms on the take back. Think: "Left arm, then right arm" (if right handed).

LEARN FROM THE EXPERTS

Maria Sharapova uses the **foot-up technique** and will land on her left foot inside the baseline. The racket will then follow through, across the body, and decelerate. Sharapova will then recover and retain balance for the next shot.

Maria Sharapova relies on an efficient coordination chain to make maximum use of the force generated in her serve—making it one of the most powerful in women's tennis. Her explosion up to the ball, using the ground reaction force, helps her reach full extension of her legs.

In the left photo, Sharapova is still in a slightly sideways position to the net, her right hip has not yet followed round. Beginners often bring the hip through too early, resulting in a loss of balance and a serve that is too low.

Sharapova keeps the racket quite close to her back, which enables her to achieve the "power loop" or circular throwing motion. The upper arm internally rotates at high speed before the elbow is extended to make contact with the ball. At this stage, having released the ball and started the upward drive, the left arm is pulled down and tucked into the stomach and chest. This helps to slow the movement of the trunk, saving this force for the "whip" at the top of the action. Momentum has been transferred from the larger body parts to the smaller muscles of the arm.

Sharapova actually lands a little inside the baseline with this serve. Her face demonstrates the **concentration and exertion** used on a powerful serve. Notice the kick back with the right leg.

HINT

Good servers keep their ball-tossing arm very straight, and hold this arm up longer—watch the professionals. If the ball-tossing arm drops early, the player often collapses on the serve and the coordination chain goes out of sequence.

RETURN OF SERVE

In any match approximately half the points are lost or won at the return of serve. If the serve is the most important shot in the game, the return of serve is a close second. You need an ability to "read" the flight of the ball early and to execute control by using simple but reliable strokes.

The basic action of the return is similar to your normal forehand and backhand, but the playing situation is very different. Your opponent has complete control of the serve and is aiming to put you under as much pressure as possible. Returns of serve can be described as defensive or offensive.

Russian Vera Douchevina hits a forceful **return of serve**. Many returns are played from less-than-ideal positions.

Defensive return

The defensive return is played when the goal is just to get the ball into play. It can be used equally against a hard, powerful first serve or a wide-angled second serve. The aim is to get the ball back into court, deep if your opponent stays back or at his or her feet if he or she comes into the net.

Offensive return

The offensive, or attacking, return is played when you are trying to take control of the point from this shot onward. It can be used against a weaker first or second serve, when you are in a position to put your opponent under pressure. You may take the ball early or may even have time to run around your backhand and hit an aggressive forehand return, either down the line or cross-court.

Tactically, there are several advantages to playing the return aggressively and taking the ball early:

• you will give the server less time to recover from his or her serve;
• you will generate pace;
• you will have more time to get to the net;
• you should have greater accuracy on your return shot because you are closer to the returning target.

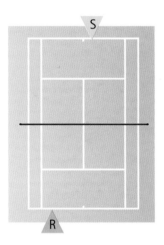

Returning serve from the **deuce court**.

Returning serve from the **advantage court**.

Forehand return of serve

• start from your ready position. Your position on the court will depend on the position of the server;
• aim to vary your court position—in order to confuse your opponent and to adapt to his or her strengths and weaknesses. If the serve is very strong, you can alter your position and stand farther back to give yourself more time;
• by moving to your left or right, you can force the ball to your stronger side.

> **HINT**
>
> You do not need to be passive when receiving serve. Try to influence your opponent by where you stand on the court or by your body language.

RETURN OF SERVE

Ready position
• start with the grip you prefer but be prepared to change it as you decide what shot you need to play.

Preparation and backswing
• get active and ready for the return when your opponent tosses the ball to serve. He or she will be looking up at the ball as he tosses it, so will not notice what you are doing;

• when your opponent is about to strike the ball, perform a "split-step" (spring your feet apart into a wide stance and keep your body relatively low) so that you can move in the direction in which the ball is coming—in this instance to the forehand side. The split step enables you to store elastic energy in your thigh muscles, which in turn will assist your own movement toward the ball.

Land from your **split-step** in a wide stance and keep a relatively low body position.

When you begin your **"unit"** turn (upper and lower body working together), use your non-hitting hand to support the take back of the racket. Look straight down the court at the oncoming ball to maintain balance and posture.

When you get into your **loading position** you should be in an open stance. Your knees should be bent and your hips, back, and shoulders poised for the shot. Keep your center of gravity low to maintain balance.

Forward swing and contact
- when hitting a defensive return, the forward swing will be similar to that of a volley (from low to high or a straight path from back to forward). Make the point of contact slightly farther in front of your body. Keep the swing compact and the grip firm;
- when hitting an offensive return, try and have a forward swing similar to your topspin forehand. Your point of contact may be higher than for your normal forehand, because the second serve is likely to bounce higher (if a topspin serve). In the illustrations you can see how the player has used numerous body parts in her coordination chain to get speed on the ball.

Follow through
- depending on the pace of the serve, the follow through with the defensive return is likely to be similar to that for a blocked volley, that is, short and compact.

Ensure your weight is **shifting forward** as you follow through. Your body should uncoil quickly so that the racket can wrap around the body as you finish the stroke. You will then be balanced and ready to recover for the next shot.

When returning a fast serve, the **take back** needs to be much more compact than for your usual forehand. The energy in your shot will mostly come from the energy stored by your loading position. Your forward swing should be from low to high. Even if you spring off the ground, your solid loading position will enable you to stay well balanced.

HINT

If returning a powerful first serve, prepare early and keep your take back short. Think aggressively on the return of the second serve.

RETURN OF SERVE

Backhand return of serve
This shot can be made with one or two hands.

The one-handed backhand return of serve
You must be ready. Watch your opponent carefully, and where possible take the shot early and attack the ball. If there is time, you can run around your backhand and make the return into a forehand.

On the return of serve you may also have to make an important decision: should you play the shot that you feel most comfortable with; or should you play the shot that you think might be most effective but which might involve a higher level of risk?

If you feel comfortable with a single-handed backhand return of serve, play it with confidence. However, you may wish to develop a two-handed shot.

The two-handed backhand return of serve
One of the greatest advances in the return of serve has been the two-handed backhand. As we have seen, the second hand provides added strength, which is very useful for young players. It also makes the all-important compact take back (small loop swing) and the open stance more achievable.

Andre Agassi powers a **two-handed return** of serve.

While landing from your **split-step**, note the direction of the ball. If it is coming to your backhand, immediately begin to move the racket back on your backhand side. Keep your head still and focussed and keep your center of gravity low with your wide stance.

Take the racket back with your preferred backhand grip. In order to **keep your open stance**, shift your weight onto your left foot. With a quick turn of your shoulders, take the racket straight back with no loop.

Make sure you keep your eyes on the oncoming ball as your **upper body rotates**. Continue to keep your weight on your left foot so that you can drive from this position.

Try to **step forward** when you are about to contact the ball. Your hips and shoulders should remain synchronized with the rotation of your body, to give added strength to the movement.

If you are strong enough, you should be able to play an extended shot and **follow through the hitting zone**— even if you are reaching for a wide ball.

Continue to use your left hand to **drive the racket through** after making contact with the ball.

THE VOLLEY

Andrei Kirilenko plays a **volley** from mid-court.

The volley

Although many players are reluctant to use the volley, this is one of the easiest shots to learn because the action required is very compact. The volley is the shot you play when you hit the ball before the bounce. It is the perfect answer to the passing shot.

Before thinking about variations, you should try to perfect the basic forehand and backhand volleys, and the drive volley. The drive volley is used more in the women's game, and it has recently been favored by many top players as an attacking, point-winning shot.

The basic grip for the volley is the continental grip. In order to have one grip for net play, you can use this grip for the forehand and backhand volley as well as for the smash shot.

When thinking about so many other factors in your game, it is easy to neglect your grip. The **continental grip** is the basic grip for the volley.

When **preparing to volley**, position your elbows in front of your body and adopt a wide stance.

Step forward with your opposing foot as you move in to volley.

The forehand volley

• start from your ready position, 6–10ft (2–3m) from the net;
• hold the racket head up in front of your body. A good tip is to concentrate on having your elbows in front of your body for flexibility of movement;
• get into a balanced position for the volley by using the split-step movement—take a small jump, then land in a wide stance. Do this as your opponent is about to strike the ball. From this position you are then able to spring into action easily, in any direction;
• use your non-hitting hand to support the racket and to initiate a slight shoulder turn;
• the key to hitting a successful volley is to move in on the ball, contacting it at a comfortable distance to the side of and in front of your body;
• as you move in, step forward with your left foot (if right handed), but do not place the foot down until after contact has been

made with the ball. This will ensure that you are well balanced throughout the volley;
• ensure that your take back and follow through are compact;
• make the path of the racket on the forward swing down and forward, with a slightly open racket face. This will impart some backspin onto the ball;
• as you follow through, move your racket forward and downward and ensure you push through the ball, keeping the racket almost parallel with the net;
• use your non-hitting arm to aid balance and therefore recovery;
• return to your ready position as quickly as you can.

> ### HINT
>
> It is important to get used to a compact take back and follow through when playing a volley. Concentrate on this in the early stages of learning the shot.

THE VOLLEY

British player Tim Henman plays a **backhand volley** at the net.

The backhand volley

The backhand volley is generally played with one hand, with the exception of the drive volley variation, which we will look at in the next section. Many of the most successful players use a one-handed backhand volley because this allows them greater reach:

• in the ready position, start with your continental grip and your racket held out in front of you;
• use the split-step movement as your opponent is about to strike the ball;
• use your free hand to guide the racket back, rotating your shoulders slightly;
• as you move onto the ball, step forward with your right foot (if right handed) and move the non-hitting hand out behind you. This hand acts as a counterbalance;
• ensure that your take back and follow through are compact;
• recover to your ready position quickly.

Make contact with the ball at a **comfortable distance**, to the side of and well out in front of your body.

The **non-hitting hand** acts as a counterbalance to the movement in the shot. It should move out behind you as you move onto the ball.

The drive volley

This volley is an important shot to learn because it is widely used—particularly in the women's game, where it is often more popular than the basic volley. The drive volley is an attacking shot and is usually played from mid-court against a slow, high-looping ball:

- select your preferred forehand or backhand grip;
- play the shot at shoulder height—the drive volley is hit on the move;
- in order to keep the ball in court, impart topspin on the ball;
- make your follow through long;
- when you have played the drive volley, move into the net to be in a dominant position in case your opponent gets the ball back.

The **drive volley**—forehand and backhand—is a combination of a ground stroke drive and a basic volley.

The low volley

The low volley is one of the hardest volleys to play. Your opponent is directing the ball to your feet, forcing you to play the ball upward. This is generally a defensive volley, but you can turn it into an attacking shot if you can play it deep, to the baseline.

- use the same continental grip as for your basic volley;
- bend and get down to the ball—make sure you bend with your knees and not from your waist or back. As you do this, your upper body will lean forward;

- make contact with the ball when it is well out in front of your body, and with a slightly open racket face. Keep your wrist firm but flexible;
- the forward swing will be from low to high, so impart some backspin on the ball to ensure you do not hit it out of the court. This shot requires good touch and careful control of the ball;
- follow through with a low-to-high movement, following the path you would like the ball to take;
- recover quickly to your ready position.

The key to a good low volley is to maintain your balance while you bend down to the ball. Try to keep your head still, because this will aid your balance. You should concentrate more on control and placement of the ball than on power.

When playing the **low volley**, bent knees, not a bent back, are important for correct technique.

THE VOLLEY

The half volley

If you have ever struggled to advance to the net in time to play a shot, you may have played the half volley, that is, making contact with the ball just as it leaves the ground from the bounce.

The half volley can also be played from the back of the court, particularly if you are trying to take the ball early to raise the pace of the rally:

• play the half volley slightly sideways on, in more of a square stance. Your take back should be reduced;

• bend your knees to get down to the ball, particularly bending your back knee, because this will stop you leaning forward too much;

• move your racket forward and with a trajectory almost parallel to the ground, depending on how close you are to the net;

• make contact with the ball in front of your body, at about ankle height;

• stay down over the ball as you follow through, moving the racket in a low-to-high path. Aim to use a little topspin, because this will help you control the ball and avoid hitting it out of court.

If you make the effort to **bend the knees and get down low**, you will have much greater control.

The **half volley**, on the backhand, prior to contact.

The lob volley

As the name suggests, the lob volley is a combination of a lob and a volley. It can be used very effectively, particularly in a doubles situation when all four players are at the net. However, you must be careful not to set your opponent up with an easy smash! In singles, the lob volley can be used after a drop shot has been played if you follow your shot into the net:

• select your typical volley grip;

• take a short backswing, opening the racket face slightly at contact;

• keep your wrist firm and play the shot with some backspin;

• make your follow through travel from low to high;

• ensure you have good touch and control for this shot, to avoid hitting out wildly.

The lob volley needs **good touch** and a feel for the ball on the racket.

The drop volley

You should play a drop volley when the ball is net height or below. This gentle, tactical shot requires great touch and control:

• use the same grip as for your volleys;

• hardly move your racket head back before contact with the ball;

• hit the ball with a very limited movement, almost as if you are simply "cushioning" the ball on the racket head;

• ensure your follow through is as compact as the take back;

• aim for the ball to land just over the net, so impart some backspin on the ball for extra effect.

The stop volley

This is often played in response to a higher and harder ball when you are close to the net. As the word "stop" suggests, this volley acts to control the ball and absorb its power and speed:

• limit your take back, because you are likely to have little time against a fast ball. This shot has more of a "blocking" action than a swing-and-hit action;

• on contact, relax the wrist and forearm to control the speed of the rebounding ball;

• keep your racket face slightly open;

• make the follow through very short, before recovering as quickly as possible.

The **cushioning effect** enables you to hit the ball just the other side of the net.

The closer you are to the net the less time you will have to respond to the ball, so you must be on your toes and have the racket head held ready.

HINT

The key to playing any type of volley is watching the ball onto the racket.

THE BASIC SMASH

The smash is the answer to the lob shot and is your chance to win the point outright. You will need good tracking skills so that you can position yourself to execute the shot effectively. In men's tennis the smash can be devastating.

The shot is generally played in the air, although there are times when you may let the ball bounce and then smash it, for example, if:

• the sun is in your eyes;
• it is very windy;
• the lob is very high;
• the lob is exceptionally deep;
• your opponent has retreated to the baseline and the bounce of the ball is high.

Using the basic smash

The smash action is similar to the serve in that it is a "throwing" action. However, in the serve you have control of the ball placement, whereas with the smash the ball trajectory is dictated by your opponent. This means you will have to move your body to achieve the positioning you need.

The grip
• use the continental grip—the same as for your volleys.

Preparation
• turn sideways and then get into a position where the ball is above and slightly to your right (if a right-handed player);
• if the ball is not very deep, use small adjusting steps (if it is very deep you will need to run back more for the smash);
• as you move backwards take the racket back, ready for the shot; when playing a smash you will usually only have time for an abbreviated take back;
• use your free hand to point up at the ball and to aid balance and coordination;
• ensure your racket head is closed (with racket strings and the palm of the hand turned slightly downwards) as it is taken back above your head;
• move the racket head down behind your head in the power loop.

A **sideways turn** is excellent preparation for the smash.

Preparing for the **basic smash** with a sideways stance...

Forward swing and contact
- throw the racket head up to meet the ball at maximum height;
- ensure that your forearm and elbow are extended at contact;
- ensure the contact point is in front of your head, with your arm fully extended upward;
- transfer your weight onto your front leg;
- as the racket moves up to strike the ball, move the non-hitting arm downward and tuck it into your stomach to help balance.

Follow through
- make your racket follow through slightly across the body to help you to recover for the next shot;
- ensure your upper body follows the trajectory of the ball and bends forward.

...the racket curving slightly across the body in the follow through.

...eyes on the ball and ready to play at the maximum height...

...contact point in front of your body...

<hr />

HINT

The key to a good smash is having quick footwork so you get back and underneath the ball in time.

SMASH VARIATIONS

Andre Agassi plays a **jump smash** from near the back of the court.

There are several variations to the basic smash. Among these are the jump smash, the backhand smash, and the bounce smash.

The jump smash
If you are faced with a very deep lob then you may want to try the jump smash, but it does need a lot of coordination. You will find that your follow through is not as long as for the basic smash:

• move to the ball very quickly, using a crossover or running action;
• get into position to take off from the ground with the rear leg. Make a "scissors" movement in the air with your legs to keep balanced;
• contact the ball in the air and then move your non-hitting arm downwards so you can get the shoulder-over-shoulder action;
• land on your rear foot, with your front foot pointing forward;
• then get into position for the next shot.

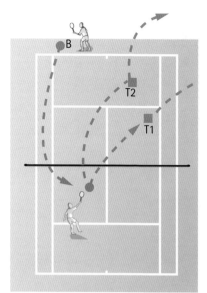

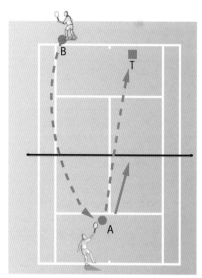

The **key to a successful smash shot** is where you hit it to. Your tactics should respond to the shot your opponent has played. If the lob played to you is short, you should angle your smash away from your opponent, directing it toward the opposite corner of the court (T1) or bounce it high over the opponent and fence (T2).

If the lob played to you is deep, aim your smash cross court and toward the middle (T), for the best margin of error. You should then close in on the net to be in a powerful position should your opponent manage to return the ball.

The backhand smash

Most opponents will try and lob to your backhand side, which is generally the weaker one. If you have time, you should move around the ball and play a normal forehand smash, but if you are forced into the backhand smash do it using your backhand grip or continental grip. This shot is great fun to practice:

• turn sideways and sidestep back and under the ball;
• try to get your elbow up high so the racket head can drop to about waist level;
• you will need to get a good shoulder turn;
• put your body weight onto your back foot and then take off from the ground with the back leg;
• try to contact the ball in front of your body with your racket head slightly forward;
• after you have made contact, swing your arm in the direction of the shot.

The bounce smash

Finally there is the bounce smash. If you wait for a lobbed ball to bounce, remember that it will not bounce straight up—you will need to move back behind the ball:

• give yourself space and then play your normal smash;
• if you are very far back in the court, hit the bounce smash with some slice in order to help control the ball.

HINT

Although pace is important, it is the direction of the smash that wins points. Think carefully about your placement.

THE DROP SHOT

The drop shot is often referred to as a "touch" shot, because it requires soft hands and careful control of the ball. Tactically, you should use this shot to force your opponent forwards towards the net. It is especially effective on clay or other slow courts, although it can also be useful on grass.

The drop shot is most effective when you have pushed your opponent well behind the baseline, and played off a slightly shorter ball although at the top level, players with good "touch" play from further back in the court. Often it is the surprise element of using this shot that wins the point, rather than the placement of the ball.

Russian Marat Safin has here been forced to **charge forward** in an effort to reach a drop shot.

Using the drop shot

You will need to get a feel for how much force to apply with the racket, and for how to absorb the pace of the oncoming ball so that you can hit a drop shot. When executing this shot your aim should be for the second ball bounce to be as near to the net as possible. This requires backspin or sidespin on the ball.

The backspin, or underspin, on the ball means that it will spin in the opposite direction to when it was coming to you. When the ball bounces, it will grip the court and rebound at a sharp angle. This is particularly useful against a player who relies on all-court attacking forehands, is slow to move forward, slow to read the ball, or who does not like volleying. Use of the drop shot can break up his or her rhythm and therefore the strength of his or her game.

It is useful to work on your drop shot early in the development of your game, because it will develop your feel for the ball and how to control it. You will also become more aware of touch and timing.

The **ability to disguise** your intended shot is important, so your opponent may be misled into thinking you are about to play a standard shot.

To play a successful drop shot, it is crucial to relax the muscle tension in your forearm and hand at the point of contact. A fun way to practice this is by playing the "game of touch" close to the net—playing only drop shots, angles, and drop volleys in the service box.

The grip
• often players find it easier to use a continental grip for the drop shot, but if you can play this shot with your normal forehand or backhand grip you will retain the surprise element of the shot.

"Soft" hands and racket face under the ball are key to a good drop shot.

Preparation and backswing
• try and prepare as you would for your normal forehand and backhand so that you can disguise the shot;
• adopt the same stance that you would for your forehand or backhand;
• generally, play the drop shot from inside the court so the ball has less far to travel. This will give your opponent less time to get to the ball.

Forward swing and contact
• use a similar forward swing to that for your forehand or backhand;
• you need a downward swing but reduce the speed of the racket head so you can get control of the ball;

• open your racket face on contact. Keep your wrist loose and bring the racket face underneath the ball, putting spin on it;
• contact the ball just before or when it reaches the highest point of its bounce;
• play the shot delicately so that you are in touch with the ball.

Follow through
• keep your follow through short, finishing at approximately waist height;
• ensure your racket face is kept open;
• ensure you keep your head still and you maintain your balance;
• on completion of the shot, follow the ball to the net so that you can reduce the angle of your opponent's return. For your opponent a tactical option is to return with a drop shot, so you need to be in a flexible position to avoid being caught out.

Having played your shot you need to recover quickly in case your opponent can make a return.

HINT

The drop shot should not be overused. It is best delivered when your opponent is not expecting it. If you can disguise your drop shot too, then so much the better!

THE DEFENSIVE LOB

The lob is played both as a defensive shot and an attacking one. In defense, this shot allows you to buy some time if you are in an awkward position. In attack, the topspin lob can force an awkward stretch for an opponent playing at the net, or result in a very high-bouncing ball that will be difficult for your opponent to retrieve or control.

American Anne White plays a **defensive lob** from the back of the court at the Wimbledon championships. White caused a stir with this one-piece outfit—the style didn't catch on.

Using the defensive lob

The basic, defensive lob is generally played when you are out of position and you need to buy time to recover. Tactically, you aim to give your opponent a high, deep smash. You may also use the lob to vary the pace of the game when playing from the baseline. A lob shot will take the pace off the ball and put pressure on your opponent to break up his or her standard baseline game. This may encourage a forced shot and produce an error.

A **low-to-high swing** and slightly open racket face are essential in a defensive lob.

The grip

• use the same grips as you do for your forehand and backhand shots.

Preparation and backswing

• prepare as if you were hitting a ground stroke (i.e., after the bounce). Your take back may be slightly shorter, however;
• bring the racket head below the height of the ball and at the same time bend well at your knees;
• open the racket face slightly;
• rest your weight on your back foot.

Forward swing and contact

• bring the racket forward in a low-to-high swing. As you do this you will gradually extend your knees forward and upward;
• ensure the racket face is slightly open.

Follow through

• make the path of the racket on the basic lob from low to high. You may exaggerate the follow through upwards, to give the ball height over the net;
• try to finish with the racket above your head height.

If you are playing the lob defensively, hit with more slice and give the ball a lot of height. The defensive lob is similar to your slice forehand or backhand. If under extreme pressure, open the racket face more and hit a very high lob to allow yourself time to recover and to read your opponent's reaction.

> **HINT**
>
> The defensive lob is a great opportunity to buy time if you are in a vulnerable position on the court and need to recover.

THE ATTACKING LOB

The attacking lob should be played with topspin. Topspin helps to bring the ball down from the lob, reducing your chances of hitting the ball out. After contact with the ground, the spin will help the ball travel forward so the net player then has farther to run to retrieve the ball.

Using the attacking lob
The topspin makes it more difficult for your opponent to smash, because it is harder to time the ball as it drops.

The grip
• use the same grip as for your topspin forehand and backhand ground strokes.

Preparation and backswing
• prepare as if you were hitting a normal topspin forehand or backhand, but bring the racket head below the height of the ball;
• ensure you have the racket face closed at the back;
• your weight will usually be resting on your back foot.

Moroccan Hicham Arazi at the Australian Open, running to the back of the court to try to retrieve an **attacking lob**. Modern players not only place the ball over their opponent's head but play the shot with topspin so it bounces fiercely away on impact with the surface.

Forward swing and contact
• try and bring the racket head up from below the ball with a brisk upward action. You need to accelerate the racket head up and through the ball;
• at contact, ensure your racket face is almost perpendicular to the ground;
• keep your wrist loose and relaxed so you can achieve good racket-head speed.

Follow through
• ensure your follow through is upward and forward, with a sharp low-to-high action;
• finish with your racket positioned well above your head.

The forward swing on the **attacking lob**...   ...just prior to contact point...   ...and follow through.

DEFENDING AND ATTACKING

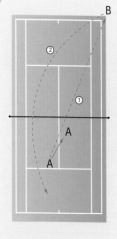

If your opponent's (A) lob pushes you deep or wide off the court, play a high defensive lob to the largest area of the court to give yourself time to recover.

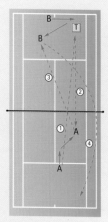

If your opponent (A) approaches to your backhand (1), hit past him or her low and down the line (2). If your opponent volleys to the open court (3) and then closes in on the net, hit an attacking topspin lob cross court to the largest space in the court (4).

USING PACE AND SPIN

Pace

As a tennis player you will often hear the word "pace," but do you know what is meant by it? Does it refer to the pace of the ball (a slow ball, a skidding ball, a high ball, a kicking ball), the pace of the court, or a combination of these?

As we have seen, on different surfaces the ball will behave differently in two ways:
• speed of bounce;
• direction of bounce.

As a player, you need to recognize these elements of pace in various situations, so that you can be prepared:

• on slow-paced surfaces, such as clay, the ball rebounds at a higher angle and at a slower speed;
• on medium-paced surfaces, such as an acrylic hard court, the ball rebounds at a normal angle and at a medium speed;
• on fast-paced surfaces, such as grass or indoor carpet, the ball rebounds at a lower angle and travels at a high speed.

In the game of tennis, you can make the most of these characteristics. By using what you know about the various surfaces, you can enhance techniques that you use on the ball—such as spin.

Different surfaces provide different **bounce and pace**. The faster, grass court shot, will bounce lower than the slower, clay court shot.

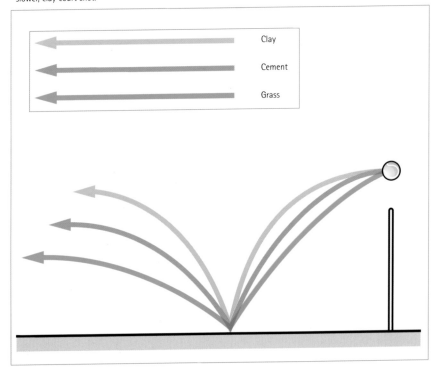

Spin

As you become a more proficient tennis player you will learn to apply spin to shots. In order to impart spin on the ball, you must accelerate the racket head on contact, to brush the back side of the ball and cause it to spin in the desired direction. The main types of spin are topspin and slice.

Topspin

Topspin involves brushing the ball in an upward direction, causing the ball to rotate forward as it travels through the air. This will cause the ball to dip—meaning you can hit the ball hard but keep it in court. The ball will bounce fast and upward, making it difficult for your opponent to return.

With **topspin** the air moves under and over the ball.

In order to perfect the topspin in a ground stroke, you should:
- prepare as for your basic forehand or backhand;
- bring the racket head below ball height and brush vertically up the back of the ball;
- the faster your racket head travels, the greater the amount of topspin you can impart onto the ball;
- when you follow through, be sure to extend through the ball before turning the racket head over.

You may notice that a lot of the top players who hit with **heavy topspin** on slow courts follow through in front of their body, using their wrists as the last link in the coordination chain. Rafael Nadal does this to great effect.

On the backhand side, if you are a one-handed player you may find it easier to put greater topspin on the ball by using a more pronounced backhand grip. This will also make it easier to hit higher-bouncing balls, where topspin is a useful weapon.

If playing a two-handed backhand with topspin, it may be more convenient to adopt a more pronounced eastern backhand grip.

125

USING PACE AND SPIN

Slice

Slicing a shot involves brushing downward on the backside of the ball, causing it to rotate backward as it travels. Slice (or the underspin shot) is used more often for control, although it can also be utilized to give an awkward bounce to the ball.

Using the slice shot

Normally you would use slice on the backhand side to try and keep the ball low over the net and get the ball to stay low on bouncing:

• prepare with your racket held higher than for your usual forehand or backhand;
• on contact, strike the back side of the ball in a downward movement;
• as you follow through, move your racket from high to low.

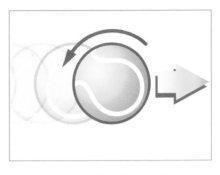

The **downward chop** on the back of the ball produces the slice.

Keep the **racket high** during preparation.

USING SPIN AND PACE EFFECTIVELY

Tactically, if you can vary the spin that you put on the ball, you will then be able to prevent your opponent from developing a rhythm to his or her shots. Alternatively, you can use spin to disrupt the rhythm or pace of a rally.

If you play against an opponent who favors speed, then you will need to vary your shots to prevent him or her from dominating the pace. Conversely, if you play against a slow and steady player, you may need to generate the pace yourself!

You can also use spin to open up the court. Move your opponent around by giving unexpected direction to the ball. You can bring your opponent forward from the baseline using a short slice shot, then play your next shot back behind him or her.

This tactic can also be applied in the serve. If you slice or topspin the serve out wide, you will drive your opponent off the court. He or she will then struggle to reach a shot played into the open space.

Jennifer Capriati volleying. When you volley you will need to put some backspin on the ball, which will help to keep it low.

IMPROVISED SHOTS

When playing tennis, you will often find yourself in a situation in which you have to compromise or improvise the shot you play. Have you ever marveled at how the professionals chase a seemingly hopeless cause on the lob, then manage to hit the ball from between their legs?

Here we will explore a few ways to practice being versatile.

The squash shot

This shot, if played well, will give you a chance to stay in the point following a very wide ball hit to your forehand side—when you are on the run and playing under extreme pressure.

In order to play the squash shot:
• change your grip to a continental or eastern forehand grip;
• take your racket back above head height;
• hack down severely on the ball with an open racket face, creating vicious underspin on the ball;
• stretch out with your right leg, if a right-handed player. On a clay court it is possible to slide into this position.

You can practice the squash shot by drop-hitting some balls yourself:
• stand deep in the forehand corner;
• drop-feed the ball and stretch out with your right leg (if right handed);
• take the racket head above your shoulder;
• hit down and through the ball as if doing a slice forehand.

You will need to use your arm and wrist to generate power. Try to direct the ball low over the net and deep into the court. Once you have gained confidence with this shot, ask a partner or your coach to feed you some balls from the other side of the net, wide and deep to your forehand side.

Preparation for the
squash shot...

...the contact point (with eyes on the ball)...

...and follow through.

Argentinian David Nalbandian surprises his opponent, and delights the crowd, with this **between-the-legs return.**

The between-the-legs shot

This is always a crowd-pleasing shot—and it is sometimes played only for show! Often, however, this shot is an option when you do not have enough time to get into the correct position to play another shot properly. If you are forced into an improvised shot you might as well play it effectively.

You will need to get into a position that allows the ball to pass between your legs. If you watch professionals do this, you will see that they run directly at the ball, then overrun it so it is right between the legs on contact:

• lift the racket above your head, using a more flexible continental or eastern backhand grip;
• bring the racket head downward to the contact zone;
• hit the ball at shin or ankle height before it bounces twice;
• follow through with a short, upward movement between your legs. Often you will jump up slightly as you contact the ball.

If you follow through with a slight low-to-high action, you can drive the ball. If you snap more severely upward, you will produce more of a defensive lob. Practice these variations by drop-hitting a ball in between your legs, then try running back for the ball and playing the shot.

With the **between-the-legs shot,** the back leg comes off the ground to allow more space for the stroke.

IMPROVISED SHOTS

Playing backwards to the side of the body
You may need to play backwards if you have
to run back to a deep ball:
• position yourself to the side of the ball
on the forehand side;
• as you run back to receive the ball,
prepare with your racket above
your head;
• bring the racket down in a pendulum
movement and contact the ball at knee
height, before it bounces twice;
• keep your wrist loose as you follow
through with an upward movement.

Practice this by standing with your
back to the net, dropping the ball to your
forehand side and attempting the shot.

Once you have mastered this drill, ask
a partner or your coach to lob the ball
over your head so that you can run back
and try the shot in play.

The jump two-handed backhand
Some professional players use this shot to
play a high backhand. Instead of moving
their feet to get into a better position,
they jump off the ground to hit the ball.
Some players like to copy this, because it
is impressive to watch, but the technical
advantages are questionable. You may find
you can get more power into the shot from
a higher angle:
• play the shot on the move, with the ball
level with your shoulders;
• jump off with your front leg while lifting
your back leg;
• start your swing as you come off the
ground and then contact the ball at the
top of your jump;
• while you are in the air, complete your
stroke with a fully extended follow
through before landing and recovering.

Playing **backwards**

The **jump backhand** is great for punching away winners
with limited backswing.

The jump or "slam-dunk" smash

Sometimes a very high lob requires an extreme maneuver in order to return the ball. If you are fairly athletic, instead of moving backward you might decide to jump off the ground to intercept the ball, with a dramatic smash. This can take your opponent by surprise—and also looks very impressive! Pete Sampras perfected his slam dunk and so became known for this shot.

In order to play the slam dunk well you must have the time to jump. The racket swing is the same as for your regular smash, but you will also need to get off the ground at the right time so that you are fully extended as you hit the ball. The shot itself needs to be a powerful flick action, because the ball must be angled down farther than usual. When you are in a position to hit the ball, pronate your forearm and really snap your wrist over so that you can slam dunk the ball into the court. You can practice this shot easily by tossing balls for yourself and then leaping to hit them.

The Sampras **slam dunk**.

Australian Pat Cash dives to make a **volley** return. Dives are more sensible on grass than on clay or other hard courts.

> **HINT**
>
> Timing is crucial with any of these improvised shots. Try to get used to timing your running and jumping toward extreme balls.

PROBLEMS WITH YOUR SHOTS

Most points are won through errors—whether unforced or forced—rather than by hitting winners. Some errors are caused by poor technique, others by wrong shot selection. Yet more errors might be triggered by poor movement (physical) and through being too tense (mental).

Here we will look at some common errors, mainly technical, and discuss some ways to overcome your problems. Your coach can help you with this; alternatively, if you can get a friend to video you, you can observe your shots yourself.

Trouble with your serve

Confidence springs from having a good serve. A good serve will immediately put your opponent on the defensive. If you can hold your serve, that is, win your service games, you will be very hard to beat. Indeed you can only lose on a tie-break. So, if your serve is letting you down, get to work on it quickly.

If you are hitting the serve into the net
• try concentrating on keeping your head up and still;
• check whether your ball toss is high enough. Try altering the height;
• ensure you drive up to the ball and contact it at its highest point;
• try keeping your ball-tossing arm up slightly longer, to help pull yourself up to the ball. If the arm drops too early, your head may drop too, causing the ball to travel too low;
• make sure you are not bringing your hip and back foot forward too early. If this is the case, the chances are that you will put the serve in the net.

If you are hitting the serve long
• check where your ball toss is and try putting it slightly farther in front of you;
• ensure you are not hitting the ball when it has fallen too low;
• perhaps you have a forehand grip—progress this to a continental one and then add a little spin on the ball.

If your serve lacks power
• perhaps you need to use your legs more. Try bending at the knees and then really driving upward;
• check your coordination chain—are your body movements synchronized?
• try generating more racket-head speed;
• ensure you get into a good loading position. Is your left shoulder higher than your right (if a right-handed player)?

If you keep foot-faulting
• ensure you keep the front foot still. Practice with a racket-head cover on your foot to stop it moving;
• if foot-faulting with the back foot, try and concentrate on keeping this foot still. Again, you could put something on your foot to prevent it moving. If the back foot is coming round the side, then practice bringing it up behind the front foot.

If you have difficulty with the ball toss
• check how you are releasing the ball from your hand if you are struggling to get a consistent ball toss;
• hold the ball in your fingertips and thumb and release it at roughly shoulder height;
• ensure your arm moves straight up in front of you;
• try not to flick the ball out of your fingers.

HINT

Video tape your shots that are causing a problem. Play them in slow motion and get the coach to help analyze them. The video does not lie!

BACK TO BASICS

Curing problems is all about getting back to doing the right things. You will need to remember what you have learned, and what works for you.

One technique is to imagine a very good shot and think about one or two simple things only. Don't clutter your mind with dozens of bits of advice; deal with one thing at a time. Visualize your service and focus on just two points that you think are important, for example:

- the kind of serve that is needed at this stage of the game;
- your routine for a good ball toss.

Appropriate grip

Place-up arm straight

Good loading position for start of coordination chain

Correct position of feet

PROBLEMS WITH YOUR SHOTS

Trouble with your return of serve
Now that you are getting more serves in court, the next most important shot is the return. If you can blunt your opponent's attack with good returns, then you will quickly win a psychological advantage.

If your return keeps going wide
• you may be contacting the ball late. Try to get a comfortable distance from the ball and move your contact point farther forward;
• aim your return away from the lines and more into the middle of the court.

If your return goes into the net
• aim to give the ball more height over the net and follow through upward;
• focus on where you are directing the return, pick a target, and aim for it;
• you may need to adjust the length of your take back. Try different lengths and see what happens to your return shot.

If your return goes long
• check whether you are transferring your weight forward. If it is on your back foot, the chances are the ball will go long;
• you may need to take a few adjusting steps around the ball;
• your racket face is probably too open on contact. Try hitting with a little topspin;
• ensure your back swing is not too large.

If your timing is off
• try to adopt a more alert ready position;
• develop a routine, so that you start your feet moving as soon as your opponent tosses the ball up. Move forward and then do a split-step movement as he or she is about to strike the ball;
• focus on the ball at all times.

If you get caught with the wrong grip
• try to study your opponent and see if he or she serves more to one position than another. If he or she does, start with that grip as a default. Then if the ball comes to the other side you only have to make one grip change;
• try not to grip the racket too tightly in the ready position so you can easily change it;
• develop a routine and use the split-step movement to buy yourself time.

Trouble with ground strokes
Now you can get more serves in and your return has improved, we will look at your ground strokes. You will need to feel confident with your game, particularly on slow courts, if you are to sustain pressure in rallies.

If you lack consistency from the baseline
• try giving the ball more height when hitting it over the net;
• put some topspin on the ball to help control it;
• focus on getting into a good hitting position—not too close to the ball and not too far away. Many errors are due to poor footwork preventing you from swinging the racket properly;
• be patient—give your opponent the opportunity to make an error.

If the ball keeps going wide
• try to give yourself more margin for error by aiming within the lines on the court, rather than to them;
• work on contacting the ball farther in front of you. If you hit the ball late and too far back, it is likely to go wide;
• check that you are preparing early enough. Often late preparation will mean a late hit;
• try hitting slightly round the side of the ball when making your ground stroke.

If the ball keeps going long
• ensure that you are transferring your weight forward and through the ball. If you lean back and play too much off your back foot, you will play with an open racket face and the ball will go long;
• try to hit with some topspin to help control the ball;
• ensure your wrist is firm on contact.

If you are hitting too many balls into the net
- there is so much space above the net—use it and give the ball good net clearance;
- you may need to use your legs more and bend at the knees. If you are too upright, this may cause the ball to go into the net;
- ensure you are not hitting down on the ball with your ground strokes;
- check your swing path and ensure it is from low to high. If you close the racket face too much, the ball will go downward.

If you tend to end up too close to the ball
- concentrate on watching the flight path of the ball more carefully, so that you can judge the ball in the air and after the bounce;
- use small and accurate adjusting steps around the ball, rather than very large ones;
- remember the routine of doing a split-step each time your opponent is about to strike the ball. This will help your balance and give you plenty of moving time.

If you are frequently lunging for the ball
- practice the split-step movement to enable you to move more quickly toward the ball;
- perhaps you did not recover quickly enough from the last shot and have been caught out of position. Concentrate on reacting quickly after each shot;
- avoid leaning to the side too much. This will affect your balance and therefore slow you down.

Tennis is a **game of the mind and body**. Simply trying harder is not always the answer to problems. Generally you will need to return to basics and feel in control of your game. You can then be focussed and fueled by adrenalin—not by agitation or tension.

PROBLEMS WITH YOUR SHOTS

Trouble with your all-round game
Having mastered the baseline game you now need to be able to play your other shots from all round the court, but these can let you down. What can go wrong? And what can you do to fix the problem?

If you keep hitting the easy volley too long, wide, or in the net
• try shortening your take back and have a short, blocking action rather than a swinging one;
• try a split-step movement as your opponent hits the ball so that you are more alert and ready for the volley;
• try adopting a more alert and lower ready position;
• make sure you are keeping your wrist and grip firm on contact with the ball, and are relaxing this grip between hits;
• keep your eyes on the ball more. Watch the ball very carefully as it approaches the racket.

If your volley goes into the net or is short
• try to move onto the ball more so your weight is traveling forward;
• experiment with your grip. If you use the forehand grip and you often hit the ball down, into the net, or too short, experiment with using the continental grip;
• check the angle of your racket face. Open it slightly and then volley with a little underspin. Follow the racket through in your target direction;
• if you are struggling with a low volley, concentrate on bending more at the knees and keeping your racket face open.

If you are hitting the volley late
• check your ready position and start with your racket farther in front and elbows away from your side;
• remember to use the split-step movement as your opponent strikes the ball, to give you more time;

• make sure you are moving forward to meet the ball rather than waiting for the ball to come to you;
• experiment with your backswing. If it is too long you are likely to be late in hitting the ball.

If you are confident when at the net, but struggle when approaching
• practice moving through the approach shot and then doing a split-step as your opponent strikes the ball. This will improve your balance as you move into the volley;
• check the length of your take back. Without the split-step it often tends to lengthen, causing you to swing at the volley;
• check your movement to the approach shot. Are you facing the net too much? Are you running through the ball and then contacting it late?

Sometimes with volleys there is a temptation to be lazy, playing the shot from the wrong position. In the long term this will cause problems. Wherever possible, **get yourself into the correct position** and play the classic shot.

If you miss an easy smash completely
• keep your eye on the ball and keep your head and chin up;
• ensure you are using a shortened take back for your smash;
• concentrate on getting comfortable with the timing of your racket throw;
• experiment with your positioning. Perhaps you are not getting underneath the ball enough. You can practice this by getting under the ball and trying to catch it with your non-racket hand.

If your smash keeps going into the net
• keep your eye on the ball at all times;
• throw the racket head upward at the ball more, trying to hit it when at the highest point;
• remain sideways-on as you hit the ball. If you face the net too early, the chances are the ball will end up in the net;
• your contact point may be too far in front. Experiment with contacting the ball more directly above your body.

If your smash keeps going long
• ensure you are not letting the ball drop too low. Hit the ball when it is at the highest point;
• perhaps you are trying to hit the ball too hard. Go more for placement than power;
• try to snap your wrist over more;
• ensure your take back is short and that you are not late on the ball with too large a take-back action.

If you don't seem to get in the right place for the smash
• check how you are moving back for the ball. If it is an easy smash, then move back with side skips. If it is a deep smash, then run back for the ball while at the same time keeping your eyes on the ball. If you are trying to move backwards, this may be affecting your balance;
• you may need to track the ball more in the air. Practice getting underneath it and catching it in your non-racket hand before you move on to hitting the ball.

WORKING ON YOUR GAME

Here we have looked at some of the common errors with the basic shots. You may come across all sorts of difficulties specific to you, in which case you should consult your coach, who can work with you directly. As you progress, the errors may become more tactical then technical and perhaps even mental. If you have worked on your fitness, you will be confident that you can get to every ball!

Even **Andre Agassi** needs coaching.

PLANNING YOUR PRACTICE

Slovakian Daniela Hantuchova enjoying **practice** prior to the Wimbledon Championships in 2005.

Once you have established the basics of tennis, the quickest way to improve your skills is through practice.

Here are a few suggestions on how to get the most out of your practice sessions:
- practice how you aim to play. Be as motivated and focussed in your practice as you are in a match;
- plan your practice and set goals for yourself;
- add variety to your practice;
- adapt the practice to suit your level. If you are a beginner, then you may frequently change the activity. As you progress you may spend longer on a specific shot or pattern of play;
- always practice your strengths as well as your weaknesses;
- practice patterns of play, for example serve out wide and hit the next ball to the open court;
- use targets to help you focus on the quality of the ball you hit;
- have bursts of high-intensity activity followed by periods of lower intensity or with short breaks. This reflects the pace of a real game of tennis;
- experiment with your shots in practice. Also try some new ones.

Choosing your practice partner

Many players feel they have to practice with somebody better than themselves. This is not the case. There are many ways you can learn a lot from different practice partners:
- if playing with somebody below your level, practice on your weaknesses, try different patterns of play, and practice moving into the net;
- if playing with somebody of your level, focus on your competitive skills and work on relaxing under pressure;
- if playing with somebody better than you, ensure you keep the ball in play and play to your strengths.`

Try to vary your practice partners so that you experience different styles of play and diverse situations. If you always play with somebody better than you, you will get a complex about losing and forget how to win! Also remember that your partner wants to get something out of the practice too. You can work as a team to practice skills and talk about your difficulties.

Before you begin

No matter what you intend to practice, you should always take the trouble to warm up. It's not worth straining a muscle when just a few minutes warm-up could prevent this. Here are some tips on how to make your warm-up valuable:
- if you use the service box to warm up, then make sure you hit with "quality";
- take advantage of the fact that points do not matter. Concentrate on the things that you don't have time to think about during the match, such as preparation and your ready position;
- try and do a split-step movement each time your opponent hits the ball.

A fun game to play is "touch" tennis, in which you play out points only in the service box. You are allowed to play only drop shots, angles, drop volleys, and touch shots. The first to seven points is the winner.

HINT

A good tennis philosophy is: "Planned practice makes perfect."

PRACTICE DRILLS AND SKILLS

The drills on the next few pages take you through the different aspects of the game of tennis. It is up to you to prepare your practice regimes with your coach—if you have one—or your partners. Always aim for variety and, although you will want to focus on different aspects in each session, try to cover your whole game.

Plastic markers are good for all drills. They are better than using chalk, because they can be removed later! This set up is for ground strokes.

Practicing your serve
The serve is the one shot you have complete control over and the one shot you can practice by yourself. You just need a few balls and a court.

Serving at targets
You can practice both your first and your second serve in this way:
• when you start, have large targets, so if you are a beginner the target might be to get the serve into the service box;
• as you progress, it may be useful to serve to the forehand side and then backhand side of the court (half the service box), and then progress to smaller targets.

Play a serving game
• set yourself targets on the court;
• have two serves at each target, a first serve and a second serve;

• if either serve goes in, then the score is 15–love, but if you miss both serves then the score is love–15;
• repeat, serving to the other side;
• play a game or set against yourself.

Serving for length and accuracy
Aim for specific targets (see diagram opposite) and award a different number of points depending on which you manage to reach:
• one point if the serve goes into the box;
• two points if it lands in a designated area;
• three points if the ball lands in the designated area and the second bounce is past the baseline;
• four points if it lands in the box and the second bounce lands past the "power line," that is, 12ft (3.5m) behind the baseline;
• try ten serves from the right box and then ten serves from the left box and see what score you can reach. You can vary the scoring to suit your needs.

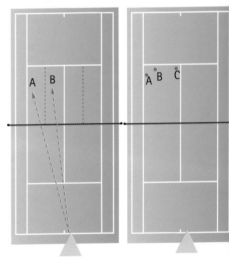

With this simple **serving game,** you try to serve to one half of the box (A) then the other (B).

A, B, and C are **serving targets.** Each is marked on court with cones or lines and is worth a different number of points. Keep score, and make sure you win!

When practicing serving for length or accuracy, award yourself the following: one point if the ball lands in the service box; two points if it is in the target areas; three points if the second bounce is over the baseline; four points if the second bounce is over the power line.

Practicing your return

Basic drill

Ask your partner to serve ten balls to each service box. See how many you can get back into court. This will help your consistency.

Drill for returning powerful serves

Get your partner to serve from the service line or just behind the service line and then try to return. You will need quick reactions.

Drill for weak second serve

Practice attacking the weaker second serve. Get your partner to hit second serves only. Move forward and practice attacking these down the line in the right court. In the left court (if you are right handed), run round the ball and play an inside-out forehand cross court, or attack the ball down the line.

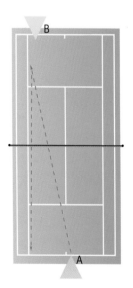

A = server
B = receiver

Attack the weaker **second serve** by hitting your return down the line.

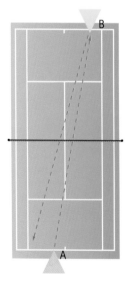

Attack the **weaker serve** cross court by running round your backhand and playing an "inside-out" forehand.

When returning **hard serves**, the server (A) can serve from on or near the service line for this drill.

PRACTICE DRILLS AND SKILLS

Practicing your ground strokes

When you play from the baseline there are five main areas to work on: consistency, length, accuracy, use of spin, and change of pace. We will look at each of these in turn and show a practice drill for each.

Consistency drills

• try to do a rally of five and then build this to 10, then 15, then 20, and so on;
• practice rallying with one ball only. This will improve not only your consistency but also your concentration levels;
• rally with your partner and see how many shots you can hit in two minutes;
• then repeat and try and beat your score.
  Obviously if you make fewer mistakes you will increase your score and also if you raise the rally tempo.

Length drills

• rally past the service line. How many balls can you get past the service line in two minutes;
• repeat and try to improve your score;
• how many consecutive balls can you get past the service line before the ball lands short, goes in the net, or lands out?

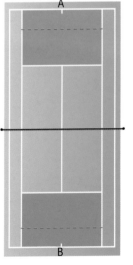

A

Get players A and B to rally into the shaded area between the service line and the baseline, or behind the red markers for more advanced players.

B

Accuracy drills

• rally cross court to a target area. Challenge yourself by ensuring that you recover just off-center in between hits. This will keep you on the move;
• to vary this drill, hit each shot with topspin and alter the pace so that no two balls in a row travel with the same pace.

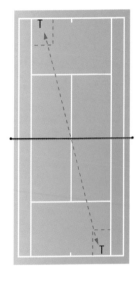

Get players to rally cross court to a special target area.

Use of spin drills

When practicing your ground strokes you need to vary the depth, angle, height, speed, and bounce of your shots, and to do this you need to impart spin on the ball. The best way to practice this is to use target areas on the court (top left diagram opposite). If you hit each ball flat, it is difficult to hit to all of these areas on the court. Try these drills:
• ask your partner to hit balls to you and then try and hit to T1, T2, and T3;
• when hitting deep to T1, try and hit the forehand with topspin and then vary the backhand. Hit some balls with topspin and some balls with slice;
• in order to hit to the short corner T2, practice both forehand and backhand with topspin and then hit some cross-court slice backhands to T2;

142

You can conveniently **mark out target areas** on the court using bright plastic markers or cones.

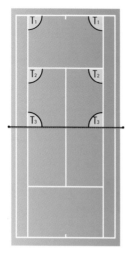

Try to hit a **slice** backhand to T1 or a shorter ball to T2. Hit with topspin to T3.

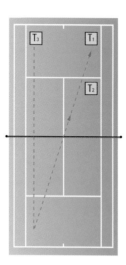

• when hitting to T3, practice the drop shot and put some backspin on the ball.

Another good drill to help you use spin on the ball is to decide an order of targets to aim for (diagram below):

• hit a cross-court forehand with topspin to T1 and then hit the next ball deep down the line to T2;

• initially try this with your partner, feeding two separate balls. Then try and build a rally, hitting balls to each of the targets in the previously decided order;

• you can play conditioned points by playing out the point once all the targets have been reached.

This drill can be varied to practice on the backhand side (top right diagram):

• hit a slice backhand cross court to T1, then on the shorter next ball hit a deep topspin to T3;

• as a variation, aim to hit a slice backhand with angle to T2, followed by a deep shot down the line to T3.

Try to hit a **cross-court forehand** to T1 and then hit the ball to T2. Play out the point against your partner or coach.

HINT

Always go on the practice court with some markers or targets and position them so they challenge your practice. It is amazing how much better you focus.

Change-of-pace drills

There is nothing more annoying than playing against an opponent who prevents you from getting into any rhythm by varying the pace of the ball. Therefore you will need to practice achieving this advantage yourself!

Using spin will help you alter the pace of a rally, but you will also need to focus on varying the height of the shots you play. Practice a drill in which you "loop" one ball and then hit the next ball flatter:

• hit the first ball with looping topspin high over the net;
• on the second ball, accelerate your racket head through the ball and hit flatter so that the ball reaches your opponent more quickly.

Also practice varying the pace on your backhand shots:

• start a rally using slice backhands cross court to your partner until you get a slightly shorter ball;
• then aim for a winning shot down the line with topspin.

Practice approaching the net

To practice your approach and first volley:
• ask your partner to hit you a short mid-court ball;
• play a deep approach shot, down the line, then come into the net and shadow the volley (play an imaginary volley) to help you with the movement forward;
• to start with, aim for the approach shot to land past the service line. As you improve you might put down a target, half way between the service line and the baseline.

Once you have mastered the movement into the net, practice playing conditioned points out on your volley:
• rally until your partner plays a shorter ball, then move in to volley.

Practice your smash

• ask your partner to feed you a series of lobs and see how many smashes you can get back and into the court.

To vary this:
• see how many smashes you can hit in a row;

• touch the net after each smash. This will make you get back to the net after the shot;
• try to alternate the direction of your smash.

Practice beating your opponent when he or she is at the net

The two key shots here are the passing shot and lob. The former will put the ball beyond your opponent's reach and can be an outright winner. The latter can have the same result, especially if played positively and well.

The passing shot

• hit a short ball, inviting your partner to approach the net;
• play the first ball to his or her feet so he or she can return it easily;
• aim to pass him or her on the second ball;
• practice passing both down the line and cross court.

The lob

• ask your partner to start at the net;
• hit the first ball to your partner who volleys the ball back deep;
• try to lob on the next ball;
• repeat ten times and then change around.

Vary the drill by trying to use the topspin lob. Remember to lob over the backhand side. A high backhand volley is harder to play than a smash if your lob is a little short.

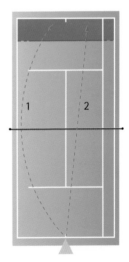

Varying the height of the ball over the net is one way to **change the pace** of a rally and prevent your opponent from getting into a rhythm.

1—looped topspin
2—harder and flatter

Conditioned points are a great way to practice in a competitive situation, while working on a specific aspect of your game. Drills such as these involve competitive play-out of a point as well as controlling particular aspects of play. Here are some ideas:

• rally cross court. When your partner hits a short ball, aim to attack this down the line. To vary this, once the ball has been hit down the line, begin to play out a point as if in a normal game;

• rally cross court for four shots, then play out the point. Beginning this drill on your backhand side will help develop consistency on your backhand;

• play out points past the service line, so that every ball has to land between the service line and the baseline;

• to practice accuracy and moving your opponent around, divide the court into four sections. Play by the rule that you must not hit two consecutive balls into the same area. This drill will test your ball control and develop your tactical awareness. There will be three options each time the ball is played. For example, if the ball lands deep in zone two, you can: Defend cross court deep to zone five; hit deep down the line to zone six; or hit an angle to zone seven.

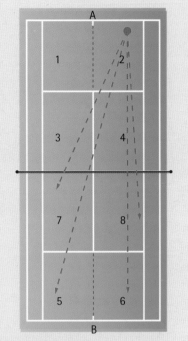

Conditioned points make practice both valuable and competitive. In this example the ball is hit into zone two. Player A then has the option to hit to zone five, zone six, or zone seven. If hit to zone eight you are asking your opponent to hit a winner!

HINT

Don't forget that you don't need to practice with somebody better than you. It can help your motivation to construct drills that help both players in a practice.

SINGLES

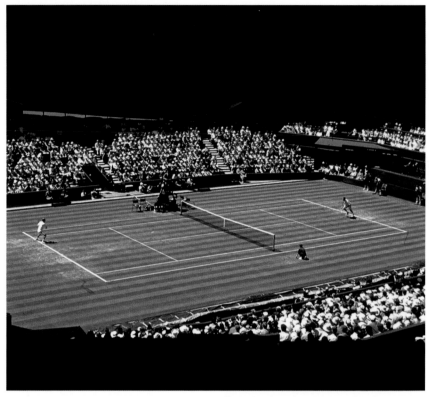

Singles is perhaps the purest form of tennis—one player is in **direct competition** with an opponent. There is no hiding place.

The game of tennis consists of four combined areas:
• technical skills—involving the key skills of the game of tennis;
• physical attributes—involving power, speed, agility, and endurance;
• mental focus—involving your competitive mindset and confidence in your own ability;
• tactical awareness—involving the strategic choices that determine the way you play your game.

Once you have your grounding in technical skills, physical conditioning, and mental focus, the remaining key component of competitive tennis is your tactical awareness. In this section we will explore

some basic singles tactics of the game, and how they form the styles of more advanced players.

There are five basic tactics in the game of tennis for all players:
• **consistency**—get the ball over the net and into court;
• **accuracy**—move your opponent around using your directional skills;
• **play to your own strengths**—use your best shots whenever possible;
• **play to your opponent's weaknesses**—this could be a technical weakness or perhaps a movement issue;
• **good recovery**—always recover quickly to a good ready position.

All tactics must be applied to the main playing situations in the game:
• when serving;
• when returning;

• when both players are on the baseline;
• when you are approaching or at the net;
• when your opponent is approaching or at the net.

Each basic tactic can be applied to each main playing situation. As an example, we will explore moving your opponent around in the various situations.

When serving
Serve wide (1) to take your opponent off court and then hit the second shot (3) into the open court.

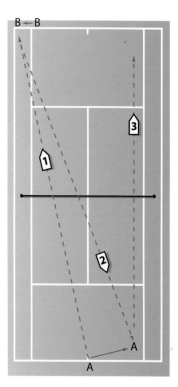

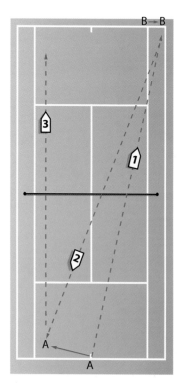

Accuracy drill when serving, from the right or left court.

Player A serves wide (1). The return is cross court (2) and player A then hits it down the line (3).

Don't underestimate the importance of footwork and recovery in between shots. The best players have great footwork and recover to a good ready position after each shot. Be ready, be alert, and don't forget the split-step!

SINGLES

Move your opponent when returning
Return deep (2) and cross court (when returning a wide serve).

Accuracy drill when returning from the **left court**.

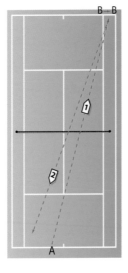

Accuracy drill when returning from the **right court**.

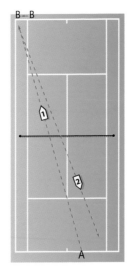

Movement when both players are on the baselines
Rally cross court and, when you (player A) get a short ball (2), move your opponent (B) around by attacking the short ball down the line (3). A strong shot will enable you to move to the net if you want to.

Accuracy drill when both players are on the baselines, from the left court.

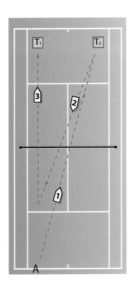

Accuracy drill when both players are on the baselines, from the right court.

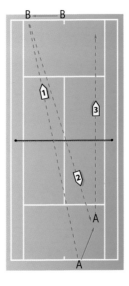

Moving your opponent when you are approaching or at the net
You (player A) should approach down the line (1) and then hit the volley cross court (3). Ideally you need a ball above net height for this volley.

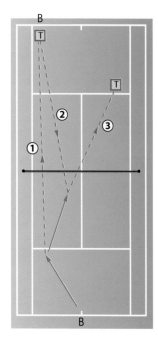

Try to be accurate when you are approaching or at the net. Aim for target areas (T).

Moving your opponent when he or she is approaching or at the net
In this situation use a lob. If your opponent (B) approaches to your backhand (1), hit a passing shot (2) down the line. If he or she volleys into the open court (3), hit a topspin lob (4) over the backhand side, forcing your opponent to turn to retrieve the ball.

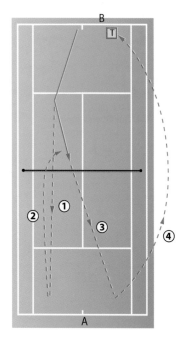

Accuracy drill when your opponent is approaching or at the net.

SINGLES

Tennis as a game of errors

Some 85 percent of points in tennis are lost as the result of an error, which means only 15 percent are genuine winning shots. Admittedly some of these errors might be forced errors!

The key to success is not only working on your real attack but also on reducing the number of errors you make and trying to force your opponent to make more. Unforced errors usually arise because of poor shot selection, faulty technique, or your bad positioning in relation to the ball.

You can develop your own tactics for reducing personal errors, bearing in mind your strengths and weaknesses. Here are some hints to help you.

Easy ways to reduce errors

Thinking about your game is a key starting point:
• how often do you play matches when the net continually "gets in the way"? There is so much space above the net, and it is only 3ft (90cm) high in the center, surely it is easier to hit it into the larger area above the net? Therefore make sure you clear the net. If you and your opponent are on the baseline, hit the ball 3–5ft (90–150cm) above the net. This will also help you to get better length on your shots;
• how often does the ball just go a few inches wide? You have a very big area to hit into! Aim the ball well inside the lines to give yourself greater margins for error;
• how often do you go for that outrageous running forehand when under pressure, only to see the ball go out? When in trouble, play a defensive shot and buy yourself some time. Aim the shot high, deep, and cross court to give yourself a chance to recover;

> **HINT**
>
> It will take time to learn the game style that is right for you. Then you can develop your tactics and patterns of play around this.

• are you the first person in the rally to change the direction of the ball? If you have hit two or three balls in a row cross court, are you inclined to hit the next one down the line? It is generally safer to hit the ball in the direction it has come from rather than changing the angle. For example, if your opponent has hit the ball cross court, the easiest return is to play it back cross court. Only change the direction when you have time and are in a good position to control the ball fully;
• how often do you make a mistake because you are not in the right position or you have not prepared early enough? Good footwork and early preparation are the key to reducing errors, and they will enable you to develop consistency.

Forcing errors

Once you can get the ball over the net and into play consistently then you need to master ways of forcing your opponent into making errors. You can:
• hit to the open court—it is impossible for your opponent to cover all the court so there will always be openings and spaces into which you can aim the ball. As soon as you hit the ball out of the reach of your opponent you will start to force him or her to run and retrieve balls and put him or her in uncomfortable positions;
• hit behind your opponent—your opponent will soon master that you are hitting into the space and start to anticipate this. If they do then hit the next ball behind them to try to wrong foot them. Hint: This is only effective against players quick at moving from side to side, if they are slow go for the open court;
• use the angles to open up the court—you need to be able to hit shots that pass over the sideline as well as the deep balls that pass over the baseline. Some players are very good at moving along the baseline but not so good when forced to move forwards and wider;
• move your opponent around—when doing this try to vary the spin and pace you put on

the ball so you challenge your opponent with every ball that you hit. It is very frustrating if you cannot get into any rhythm with your shots. Don't forget to use the length of the court as well as the width. You can force your opponent back deep behind the baseline with a high loopy shot and then play a shorter ball or drop shot to force them to move forwards;

• watch your opponent play other matches—see if you notice any weaknesses that you could then exploit when you play them. Hint: Don't play every shot to the weakness, as it may get better as the match progresses!

Remember, always try to play to your own strengths first and then exploit your opponent's weaknesses.

DEVELOPING A GAME STYLE

As you start out, you may look to professional players as role models, and try to imitate their style of game. However, it is important to develop your own game style, based on your own technical, mental, and physical characteristics. This style will then dictate the tactics you use. There are four main game styles.

The net rusher/serve and volleyer

These players are generally tall, have a powerful serve, like to volley, have a strong smash, and move forward well. They like to challenge their opponent to get the ball past them. Using speed and power-based shots, these players are more effective on fast surfaces. However, in today's game, the technical advances in the passing shot and techniques on the lob mean that not many players dare to adopt this style.

Aggressive baseliner

These players stay close to the baseline and take the ball early, using powerful ground strokes. Baseline players will often rely on at least one weapon or strength, usually the forehand, and will try and dominate the rally from the baseline using this attribute.

Counterpuncher

These players are mostly defensive, baseline players who react to their opponent. Their strengths are in reliable

return of the ball, adopting a "never-say-die" attitude. Counterpunchers will play slightly farther behind the baseline than the aggressive baseliners, mixing up the rally with varied spin on their shots. These players are generally more effective on slow courts—winning rallies through a combination of endurance and determination.

All-court player

All-court players rely on versatility, adapting to any pace and style of game, readily switching from defense to offense, and playing confidently in any area of the court. This is a strong style of play on any surface.

Leyton Hewitt is a great example of a successful counterpuncher.

DOUBLES

The Australian pairing of **Mark Woodforde and Todd Woodbridge**—the Woodies—was perhaps the most successful in the modern game. Although neither of them had major success as singles players, they did win five successive Wimbledon doubles titles and Olympic gold medals among a host of career victories.

The game of doubles is fast moving and requires smart thinking. Developing a partnership where you know what to expect from your partner in terms of fitness, power, and support is a challenge. When choosing a doubles partner, you should bear in mind your own weaknesses so that you can benefit from your partner's strengths.

Good singles players do not necessarily make good doubles players. The key components to a successful doubles partnership are:
- teamwork;
- cooperation;
- communication;
- thinking ahead.

Positioning

The most common starting positions for a
doubles team is with one player at the back
and one player at the net. However, there
are alternatives.

Both-back position

This is a very defensive position. You may
have a better chance of returning powerful
shots hit straight at you, and your opponents
will struggle to find a vulnerable space on
the court. If your team are struggling to
break serve and the net player is being
targeted, this is a wise choice of formation.

Australian formation

If you, as the server, are struggling to volley
the cross court return, try the Australian
formation. Your partner starts on the same
side of the court as your serve, so he or she
is in a good position to intercept the
returned ball as a volley. This tactic also
causes indecision in your opponents as to
where to hit the ball.

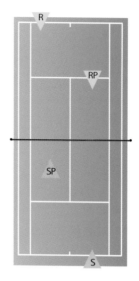

Standard doubles set up

S = server   R = returner
SP = server's partner   RP = returner's partner

In the **both-back position**, the returner and returner's
partner start on the baseline.

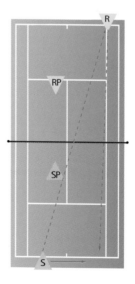

In the **Australian formation**, you should hit your shots
to whichever opponent is deeper in the court. If they
close in on the net, then use the lob.

153

DOUBLES

I–formation

In this formation your partner crouches down on the center service line, close to the net. Prior to your serve you have told your partner where you are serving to and have an agreed plan. Your partner knows whether he or she will move to the right or the left, and you will cover the other half of the court after the serve. Again, this formation makes it difficult for your opponents to choose a direction of return.

Tactics in the game

There are various tactical options that you can choose from in each element of the game.

Serve options

Always talk to your partner or use hand signals so he or she knows where you are going to serve to and can cover the appropriate area of the court:
- serve down the middle to reduce the angle of return;
- serve wide to take your opponent off the court (but be aware of the angle of return or the return down the line);
- serve to the body to "jam" your opponent.

Return options

- return cross court to your opponent's feet if he or she is serving and volleying;
- return cross court and deep if your opponent stays back;
- lob over the server's partner (aim over the backhand side). This is more effective if the opposing team is trying to serve and then attempt a volley;
- aim at the net player, especially if he or she is a weak volleyer;
- attack down the middle of the court between the two players;
- return cross court to the short angle. This is often used as a softer shot, out of the reach of the server's partner. It can either bring the server off the baseline, or if he or she is coming in it will force him or her to volley upward.

The **I-formation** is chosen for tactical reasons and needs accuracy of serve.

During play

- use the tactic of hitting down the middle between your opponents. This causes confusion as to who will take the ball. If the players then crowd the middle, the sides are open for you to play a winner;
- lob out of trouble. In doubles, this can cause confusion and frustration in the opposing team, because they are prevented from getting into an attacking rhythm;
- use an element of surprise by "poaching" your partner's shots. This simply means encroaching on the area expected to be covered by your partner, usually by intercepting the ball at the net. Poaching needs practice, and you need confidence to do this, but once you have established a pattern in your opponents' play then you can try it. Often you will see top players use hand signals before the serve to communicate where the serve is going, and whether they are going to poach or not;
- it is easiest to win points from the net in doubles, so adopting the tactic of serve and

154

The server's partner will **point his finger** to the side he would like the serve to be hit to.

He will then **indicate that he is going to poach** with his hand open, or close his fist if he is going to stay.

volleying will enable you to take the net position quickly. Serve to your opponent's weaker side, move in quickly, split-step as they strike the ball, and generally play the first volley deep. You should then move in for the second volley.

DOUBLES—DON'T FORGET

• try to get to the net before your opponents. If you are serving, then serve and volley so you can get to the net quickly. If you are returning, look to chip and charge and get into the net off the return of serve;
• aim to get a high percentage of first serves into play. If you serve down the middle, you will reduce the angles of return possible for your opponents;
• isolate the weaker player. Observe the weaker of your two opponents and aim to attack him or her where possible;

• cover and exploit the middle court. As a team you will need to work out a plan of responsibility for shots played down the center of the court. Likewise, try to hit between your opponents;
• work as a team and encourage your partner. Try not to show any frustration when your partner misses a ball and show support by encouraging him or her to go for his or her shots. Don't put pressure on your partner and reassure each other after each point is played.

HINT

There are no substitutes for knowing your partner's strengths and weaknesses, and encouraging and supporting him or her.

PERCENTAGE PLAY

James Blake plays forcefully from the baseline, keeping the pressure on his opponent.

Although it is important to practice your winning shots, it is not realistic to play perfect attacking shots all the time! "Percentage tennis" is all about compromising your shots to limit unforced errors, by playing the easiest and most efficient shot in any given situation.

A strong game depends on your shot selection. You should choose shots that will maximize your strengths and minimize your weaknesses. Shot selection will differ depending on the skill level of the player—a safe shot for one player may be a risky shot for another!

There are four basic types of shot that you can play, but you only have a split second in which to decide.

Offensive or attacking shot
Here you are trying to hit an outright winner or a shot that will really challenge your opponent. You need to be in a good position on the court with sufficient time to prepare. The shot must be at the right height and pace.

Building shot
This is a shot where you are building or setting up to control the point within the next couple of shots. It may be the first shot within a pattern that you plan to use in a particular game.

Neutralizing shot
You will need to use this when trying to neutralize a strong shot from your opponent. You are aiming to take back the advantage he or she has gained.

Defensive shot
You will require this when you are under pressure and trying to stay in the rally. Perhaps your opponent has you on the run, so that you are forced to hit a defensive lob to buy some recovery time if at all possible.

Successful percentage tennis
Playing percentage tennis that will reduce the risk in your game and encourage you to adapt to all variations of playing situation. There are some basic principles of percentage play:
• know your game style, your strengths, and your weaknesses. Do not attempt to play shots that are not in your repertoire;
• understand and recognize attacking, neutralizing, and defensive situations;
• keep the ball in play;
• give yourself a margin for error by hitting the ball into the larger spaces on court;
• give the ball height over the net on your ground strokes to reduce net errors;
• hit more shots across court. This is the longest distance you can play and the ball passes the lowest part of the net;
• use spin to keep control of the ball;
• hit to the larger court areas when hitting with power;
• think about your playing conditions and adjust to them.

Playing the percentages can readily reduce unforced errors, and many a match has been won by using this strategy. Don't try to play shots that you do not possess!

PERCENTAGE PLAY

Let's look at some examples of percentage play in a variety of game situations.

When serving
Hit your first serve at 70–80 percent of your maximum pace, rather than aiming for an ace every time. Try to dominate the game with a reliable serve, not always to end it.

When returning
If the ball is served wide, return it cross court to the server's side. In singles, if the serve is central, return it to the opposite side to the server. In each case the ball will cross the lowest part of the net, giving you more chance of getting it into court.

When both players are on the baseline
Rally cross court, hitting the ball deep with reasonable pace and good net clearance. Only change the direction of the ball when the ball is short and you are in a good position to attack it down the line.

If the ball lands in the middle of the court
Run around the ball to position yourself for a forehand, then hit to your opponent's backhand side. This pattern is adopted extensively by professionals, who try to use their strong forehand as much as possible.

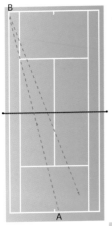

A = server
B = returner

When percentage returning, hit cross court if the ball is served wide.

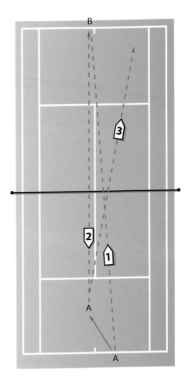

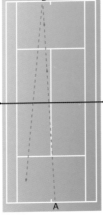

If the ball is **served down the center line**, the easiest return shot is to your opponent's backhand side. In this example, the server is right handed so the return has been made to the server's left side.

If you have the opportunity, you can run around your backhand to play a safer and possibly **more penetrating forehand** shot (3) to your opponent's backhand serve.

158

When approaching the net

The general rule is to approach the net down the line and then look to put the volley away with a sideways angle. If you approach the net cross court, you often leave too much undefended space. This makes it easy for your opponent to hit the ball past you. Your shot selection will depend on the height, pace, and spin on the mid-court ball. If the ball is low, go for more control and depth. If the ball is high, you can hit a more forceful shot.

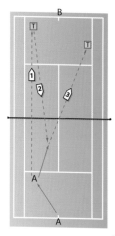

If the ball is above the net height, drive it down the line (1) and then put the volley away (3) to target area T.

If the ball is below the net, use a slice approach down the line for control and depth.

Patterns of play

Now you have an understanding of percentage play, try to develop some basic patterns of play that can help you win matches as the professionals do. You need to build these patterns around your strengths, so if your forehand is your best shot, set up patterns so you play into your forehand. If your backhand is a weakness ensure the pattern does not include a lot of backhands.

Try to master a few patterns well, rather than learn a lot only averagely.

A basic pattern on the serve
- serve out wide—this will open up the court and take your opponent off the court and then the next shot can be hit into the open court;
- if you have a serve and volley style you may serve out wide and then volley into the open court.

A pattern on the return
- neutralize your opponent—by returning the ball deep down the middle of the court, pushing your opponent back and not allowing them to attack.

Perfect certain patterns of play that you feel comfortable with and then incorporate these into your game.

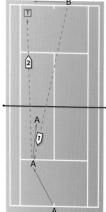

PLAYING CONDITIONS

Clay courts slow the ball down a little and tend to favor the players who can rally consistently from the baseline. Stamina and concentration are essential for success.

You need to play every game to your strengths, but you will often find that you have to adapt to variations in your playing situation. The main factors to consider are:
• type of surface;
• your opponent;
• weather conditions.

Adjusting to different surfaces: Clay

As we have seen, clay surfaces mean higher bouncing balls and longer rallies. Therefore, one of the most important tactics to use is to increase the margin of error on your shots. Don't forget most of your points will be won from your opponent's errors rather than from your own winning shots.

Give variety to your serves on a slow surface
A serve that relies on speed will struggle to be effective on a slow surface. You will need to develop a secure, heavy serve with topspin rather than rely solely on trying to hit with power. Introduce a variety of spins and angles on your serve.

Use more aggressive returns
When returning serve, you will find you have more time on a clay court so you can be more aggressive with the return. If you hit high and deep, this will force your opponent back behind the baseline.

It is difficult to serve and volley on clay, because your opponent has a lot more time to pass you. Your footing is not as secure, and it is more difficult to change direction. If your opponent does come into the net, then try and use the two-ball pass, in which you hit the first ball with dipping topspin to his or her feet and then pass or lob on the following ball.

Give the ball more height
If you watch clay-court professionals, you will see how high they hit the ball over the

net. The main advantages of giving the ball more height are to gain more depth on your shots, to reduce the risk of the ball going in the net, and to give yourself time to recover for the next shot.

Expect longer rallies from the baseline
Generally, you should hit with more topspin on clay, to force your opponent farther behind the baseline. The topspin will make the ball bounce up high on your opponent, making it difficult for him or her to hit winners off the shoulder-high balls. You then need to look for any shorter ball that you can flatten out and try to put away. Look to "wrong foot" your opponent, by hitting behind him or her.

Make your opponent run forward
Another tactic regularly employed on clay is to use the long baseline shots to push your opponent back, and then bring in a drop shot to force a sprint forward. The ball will "die" quickly on a soft clay court, so it will be hard for your opponent to reach.

When rallies are as long as on clay, it is essential to open the court up with angled shots, short balls, and drop shots.

In the mid-court you need to look to hit well-angled shots and perhaps use the drive volley to be able to put the ball away. You could hit high looping balls to your opponent's backhand and then sneak in and play the drive volley.

Adjusting to different surfaces: Medium-paced indoor or hard cement courts

On hard surfaces, the ball rebounds at a lower angle and travels at a medium speed.

Serve harder but use spin
Fast serves will be more effective on hard courts, but you will still need to use some spin to keep your opponent guessing as to your tactics. Servers often aim the ball at the receiver's body, giving him or her little time to move into a position to return.

Concentrate on defensive returns of serve
When returning you may have to block the harder serves, then look to attack anything weaker. Be prepared for that serve directed at your body.

Medium-paced courts tend to be favored by players with an all-court game, because they can rally from the baseline and then look for anything shorter to try and come to the net.

When coming into the net, look to put the ball into the open court, using short angled volleys and aggressive smashes. You will need to use a combination of shots hit with different spins and heights to outmaneuver your opponent.

Hit the ball harder and flatter
Clay surfaces suit most game styles. You will have to be ready for rallies of any duration. Hard, flat returns keep up the pressure.

Rally cross court if your opponent is quick at recovering towards the center. You can wrong foot him or her by playing the ball behind them.

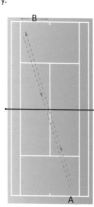

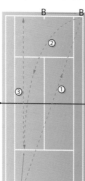

From the baseline, hit a **high looping ball** to your opponent's backhand (1). Then sneak in and play a drive volley (3).

PLAYING CONDITIONS

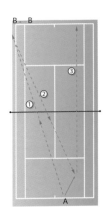

On fast-paced surfaces, slice the serve out wide (1) (if right handed) to the deuce court to take your opponent (B) off the court. Then hit the next shot into the open space (3) or back behind your opponent if he or she recovers quickly.

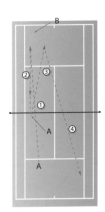

In the two-ball pass, if your opponent (A) hits a moderate approach down the line (1), on your first shot you should drive hard and low down the line (2) to force a weak volley (3) and then pass him or her on your second shot cross court (4).

Adjusting to different surfaces: Grass and fast indoor courts

On fast-paced surfaces, the ball rebounds at a lower angle and travels at high speed. You should make shot selections that make the most of these characteristics.

Use the hard, flat serve and the angled slice serve

Practice the slice serve, aimed out wide in the right court (if right handed). This will take your opponent off court, so that you can then hit the next shot into the open space or back behind your opponent.

Expect fast serves

If returning against the hard serve, shorten your take back and try playing percentage returns to give you the best chance to get the ball back. If your opponent stays back after the serve, then try to return deep. If he or she serves and then moves in to volley, try to return to his or her feet and look for the two-ball pass.

Expect shorter rallies

You should try to take control of the point from the first strike. If you are serving you will need to hit an aggressive serve and then perhaps look for the forehand attack off the third ball. If you are returning, try to hit an attacking return that puts your opponent under pressure.

Look for the short balls

If you play from the back on a fast court, the rallies are often short and the balls are hit fast and flatter. Look for any short balls and try to attack these, and then close into the net and put the ball away. If the court is really fast, then you want to think of trying to get forwards and to the net as quickly as possible, so the ball does not bounce. If you are trying to pass your opponent, try to use a variety of spins and lobs to get him or her out of position.

Adjusting to different opponents

The biggest challenge in tennis is to find your opponent's various strengths and weaknesses and nullify their style of play.

Technical

Observe each shot your opponent plays, and take note of weaknesses or common mistakes. Perhaps he or she reveals a poor backhand, in which case you should aim to take advantage of this. The warm-up is an opportunity to look at your opponent's strengths and weaknesses.

If your opponent tends to dominate on particular shots, try to avoid giving him or her the chance to play them. For example, you may aim to hit around your opponent's powerful forehand or you may concentrate on defensive returns of hard, fast serves.

Physical
You are likely to play against opponents of varying fitness and endurance. Observe how quickly your opponent tires when moving around the court, and any difficulty he or she has in stretching to wide balls. Perhaps moving your opponent from side to side will stretch his or her endurance. If he or she is particularly alert in moving around the court, but weak on power, concentrate on challenging him or her with speed.

Tactical
Less experienced opponents may be slower to read your shots, in which case using varied spin and pace will really challenge them.

If your opponent seems to predict your shots well, don't take too many risks with your tactical play.

Mental
Although this might be difficult to judge, you might notice if your opponent is timid in playing powerful ground strokes or in approaching the net. You can take advantage of these insecurities by exaggerating your attacking forehand or by playing tactical, shorter balls.

Adjusting to different weather conditions
Unfortunately, the weather is something that we cannot predict. However, it is possible that your tactics during a game of tennis will be influenced by factors such as wind, visibility, and temperature.

Wind
Wind is hard to adapt to, because it regularly changes direction. You will need to adapt each time you change ends and use your technical skills to keep the ball under control. If you are playing with the wind behind you, use your topspin to control the ball. If the wind is against you, you must use more power and follow through, aiming higher and deeper than usual.

It is possible to use the wind to your advantage in the game, as long as you don't let it affect your confidence.

Visibility
If visibility is poor, it is likely that you and your opponent will be equally affected. You could aim to use disguised spin, because these shots will be even more difficult to read in the circumstances.

If the sun is very bright, it will be in your eyes only from one end of the court. When the sun is in your opponent's eyes, challenge him or her with lobs and high, loopy balls.

Temperature
The heat can force you to alter your tactics—both you and your opponent will tire more quickly. If you are struggling with the heat you may try to shorten the rallies. Conversely, move your opponent around to tire them more. Take time in between points and at change of ends, and when possible stand in the shade. Drink water to avoid dehydration and loss of concentration.

Be prepared for everything. Here the heat has taken its toll on Anna Kournikova.

HINT

Don't be reluctant to play in situations that you are not used to. Every experience you have will improve your awareness of the game as well as your tactical repertoire.

CONTROLLING YOUR GAME

The very nature of the game of tennis ensures that it is mentally extremely tough. It is, in particular, a game of choices. As soon as you step up to the line to serve, you will need to decide where to serve to, what spin to put on the ball, how hard to hit the ball, and whether to aim for placement or power. Also if you hit to a certain direction, you will need to think about what type of return you might get—and you haven't even hit the ball yet! Tennis is a game of decisions. In addition, as tennis is an individual sport (except when playing doubles) there is nowhere to hide if you are playing badly. There are normally no time limits—you cannot play for time as in football, and you cannot bring on a substitute.

However, despite all this, there is the advantage of regular "thinking time" during a tennis match. Between points you have 20 seconds, and then 90 seconds at change of ends. It is essential that you take advantage of this time, using it positively and constructively.

Mentally tough players have great belief in their own ability. They present a strong, confident image on court and display positive body language and high energy, regardless of how they are feeling inside. They have good concentration levels and do not let their minds wander into the future or dwell on previous mistakes. They are focussed and alert, enjoy the battle, and have a great desire to win.

There are four elements to a strong mental state in tennis:
• concentration—the ability to stay focussed on the present moment;
• commitment—the drive and stamina to do whatever it takes to succeed;
• control—this will include control of your behavior and your emotions;
• confidence—the belief that you can put the ball into court in any given situation.

The serve is a good point to take stock. Don't rush it. Russian Elena Dementieva exhibits **control and focus** as she eyes the ball prior to her serve.

What can you control

Staying mentally fit in a tennis match means focusing on the elements of the game that you can control. You cannot control how well your opponent plays on the day, the weather, the net cords, or a bad line call. What you can keep in check is your own reactions to all of these. This kind of discipline is the secret of successful players, and needs to be learned and worked in the same way as fitness, technique, and tactics.

Set yourself goals

You may find that you are more concerned about winning the match than how well you perform. However, psychologically it is important not to let positive aspects of your game go unnoticed if you end up losing a match. It is possible to play the best game of your life but still lose to a more advanced player—but even a lost match can be used constructively in terms of self-appraisal. One of the key mental tools to use here is goal setting. There are two types of goal.

Outcome goals

Outcome goals are concerned with winning or losing a match. For example, you may set yourself a goal to win at least three rounds in a tournament, or simply to win in every match you play. These are targets that are not under your control and are largely dependent on your opponent, so you must try not to focus on these.

Performance goals

Performance goals are concerned with your personal skills and achievements within the game and are unaffected by whether you win or lose. For example, if you aim to increase the number of first serves you get into play by 10 percent, you can still achieve this goal even if you do not win the match.

Performance goals are under your control and can be used to boost self-awareness and confidence, and to transform even lost matches into positive playing experiences.

CHECKING YOUR PROGRESS

Before a match write down some performance goals for that match and have a pre-match plan, which will keep you focussed. You might devise a chart.

Performance goals	Achieved rating	Score
• to get 70 percent first serves into play	75 percent	10/10
• to attack mid-court balls and follow them into the net	did most of the time	7/10
• to attack opponent's second serves	about 60 percent	6/10

Comments on match
• I thought I played well and my first serve was going very well, but I felt I served too many balls out wide and my opponent took advantage of this;
• when I did follow the mid-court ball to the net I was successful, but I did not have enough confidence to do this all the time;

• I tried to attack my opponent's second serve but his topspin was causing me a few problems.

Areas to improve
• continue with my first-serve percentage and now direct and vary the serve more;
• practice following the mid-court ball in more;
• work on returning high-kicking serves.

CONTROLLING YOUR GAME

Use of routines
Another way to help you stay calm in your game is to have routines. These provide rhythm, focus your concentration, minimize your distractions and negative thoughts, increase your feelings of self-confidence and control, and ensure that you are fully prepared for each element of a match.

Pre-match routines
Pre-match routines are particularly important and cover aspects such as sleep, nutrition, and warm-up. We will look at these more closely in the next section.

Between point routines
You might observe that most top players behave in the same way in between each point they play—whether the point is won or lost. Most will include a physical response, then a relaxation response, some form of preparation, and then a ritual (for the serve or return) before the next point starts. This

is a great way to remove yourself from any negativity associated with the previous point, and to treat each point as a new opportunity.

If you practice a routine regularly, it will become automatic. For example, at the end of the point turn your back on the ball, transfer your racket into your non-playing hand and relax your playing arm, look at the strings, walk positively back and behind the baseline, and then as soon as you turn round focus on the next point.

Change of ends routine
You have 90 seconds at the change of ends and 120 seconds at the end of each set. This down time can be invaluable if it is used really constructively:
• sit down;
• towel down and dry yourself;
• have a drink;

Towelling down and adjusting racket strings are two common **rituals to keep players focussed** on the game.

The changeover time (at every odd game, 1, 3, 5, etc.) can usefully be spent in **reclaiming mental and physical strength**.

• you will either need to relax yourself or activate yourself—find some key phrases that are helpful to say to yourself;
• adjust any equipment if necessary;
• consider your tactics for the next games;
• do not dwell on any previous mistakes, but use them positively in your consideration of tactics that you should be adopting.

Try to stick to your routine. This is one element of the game that can remain constant and unaffected by the way the match is going. Avoid putting unrealistic pressure on yourself or rushing if things aren't going well.

Your state of mind in play
Emotional responses
During play, you will find that you will respond emotionally in one of four ways:
• tank—you withdraw effort and commitment so that you experience less stress. In this situation you make excuses for not trying; for example: "The courts are so bad I cannot play," "I cannot play in the wind—what's the point";
• anger—you lose your temper;
• choking—you worry unduly about the outcome of the match, to the extent that it affects your standard of play;
• fight—you relish the battle and fight for every point.

Try to be aware of these reactions and consider them after your matches. This will help you to explain any stress or negativity that you are experiencing and to learn to control your reactions to your own advantage.

Concentration
To be successful with your tennis, concentration is the most important mental skill you will need. Many factors can affect your concentration, especially if you are nervous:
• you may distract yourself by dwelling on past points played or wondering what is going to happen later in the match;

• you may distract yourself through "choking"—diverting your concentration to negative situational factors of the game;
• you may be irritated by your opponent and begin to focus on that too much;
• you may be over-analytical of your game play and lose your flow.

We have seen how goal-setting and applying routines can help refresh your focus and your self-control at various points in the match. Here are a few more techniques that may help you maintain concentration while you are playing:
• use trigger words or keys phrases such as "come on" or "ok here we go";
• focus on the ball and what it is doing—as opposed to thinking about what is going on around the court;
• use steady breathing rhythms;
• evaluate shots positively to keep your attention focussed on play;
• use visualization techniques—visualize how you are going to play the next point to keep your attention in context.

You can also practice various drills, in practice as well as in the match, to strengthen your concentration:
• try the split-step movement every time your opponent hits the ball;
• say "bounce, hit" to yourself each time you or your opponent hits the ball. If you do this, you cannot be thinking about anything else;
• breathe out at contact point and whisper a long "yes" as you hit the ball;
• when practicing, use one ball only so that if you miss it you have to go and fetch it. You will be amazed at how well you keep the ball in court;
• when practicing your serve, call out the direction of where you are aiming for prior to hitting the ball;
• while serving, ask your friends to call out and distract you by bouncing balls and moving around. Can you maintain your focus and keep a straight face?

BEFORE AND AFTER THE MATCH

In the last section we looked at how routines—especially before a match—are invaluable to alleviate stress and to exert a feeling of control and confidence.

The pre-match routine

Your routine behavior prior to a match should attend to aspects such as sleep, nutrition, organization, and physical and mental preparation. The following factors can be included in your pre-match routine, to give you complete peace of mind to concentrate on your game:

• prepare your kit the night before the match is scheduled to start;

• plan for a good night of sleep;

• check the practice court time and arrange a practice partner;

• plan when you will need to leave to get to the tournament in good time;

• check the time of your match;

• check who you are following onto court, and keep checking his or her score;

• plan what time you will need to eat prior to your match;

• ensure your drinks bottles are full and that you have a snack available should you need extra energy;

• ensure you have set your goals for the match and you have clear strategies and

Stretching on the court prior to a match may help you prepare physically as well as familiarize yourself with the court.

tactics. Focus on your performance rather than the outcome of the match;
• allow time to stretch prior to the match. Work out a stretch routine to carry out before a match. A coach or fitness instructor can help you with this;
• allow some quiet time before the match so that you are not distracted. This may include time to use visualization techniques.

Self-confidence

The greatest weapon you can take onto the court is confidence. This is something that comes from your expectations of success and failures and something you develop based on your achievements and your awareness of your own strengths and weaknesses.

You will notice that all successful players come across as strong and confident in their game. This ensures that they play to their best ability.

Confidence is about knowing that you can keep the ball in play, time after time. It can be built by a good conditioning process of practice and self-belief. You have to build positive habits of thought in your mind and your actions. You also have to believe in your shots and know that you can hit them well at all times. This is why it is so important to practice and develop confidence

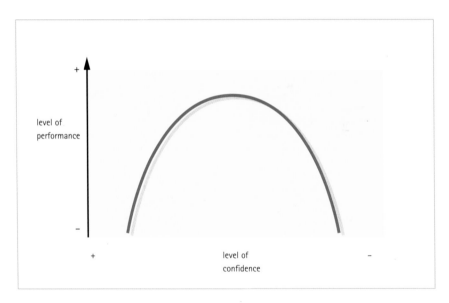

Maintaining a **high level of self-confidence** will help you play to the higher end of your ability.

HINT

Start to change all those negative thoughts you have about your tennis into positive ones—believe in yourself.

BEFORE AND AFTER THE MATCH

Your **body language** on court may help your opponent—or worry him! Two British players—Tim Henman (left) and Andy Murray (right)—react differently while under the pressure of playing at Wimbledon.

in your own strokes. A self-confident person is a believer. He or she is positive about him—or herself—but also realistic.

You can work on your confidence in the same way as you do your technique, tactics, fitness, and in-match routines.

Here are a few things you can do or consider before a match in order to boost your self-confidence:

• use positive self-talk: "I feel confident in today's game," "I've prepared well for this match and will do my best," "great shot," "keep going, you are playing well." This can be a very powerful tool;

• work on your fitness routines so that you go into a game knowing you are physically very able;

• try and display confident body language when approaching or playing on the court. Walk tall with your head up and shoulders held well back;

• think about how hard you have trained, and have pride in your ability;

• think about your role models and how they have influenced and inspired you;

• set realistic and achievable performance goals before the match;

• act decisively and trust your instincts;

• never think "what if?" or worry about repeating past mistakes before a match.

Many factors can have a negative effect on your confidence. You need to understand these things so that you do not allow them to influence your perception of your own ability. It is inevitable that you will make mistakes during a game, such as missing too many shots, losing against players rated below you, missing the easy balls, or double faulting. You must remember to evaluate these instances in a positive and constructive way. Confidence does not only come from winning matches!

After the match

It is just as important to work out a post-match routine as it is to develop routines before and during a match. This will put you in a good frame of mind to evaluate your performance in an objective and useful way:

• cool down and stretch;

• have a shower and give yourself some quiet time;

• ensure you eat after the match so that you are not assessing your performance when your energy levels are low;

• review your goals to see if you have achieved them. Focus on your own performance in the match, not on the overall outcome;

• review the match from a positive perspective and write down what you have learned from it as well as how you can improve and move your game forward;

• if you are talking to your coach, you may find it is best to do this an hour or even longer after the match, when you can think calmly and construct your thoughts without being emotional.

Analyzing your game with your coach—both before and after a match—is key to long-term development.

HINT

Remember that you only have one opponent in a game of tennis (unless you are playing doubles). Work on your preparation and your confidence so that you are not battling with yourself!

ETIQUETTE

Tennis is based on official rules that determine the structure of the games and the scoring system. However, there are many unofficial "rules" or traditions that you should respect as a tennis player. These relate to things such as your attire, your organization of play, and the interaction between you and your opponent and/or umpire. If you are known as a sporting player you will enjoy your tennis more. It is not true that you can't be competitive, successful, and well-liked. Here are some rules for you to consider.

Attending or organizing a friendly match
• if you make arrangements to play with a fellow club member, friend, or someone from another club, make sure you respect your opponent's time and be punctual and organized in your arrangements;
• come prepared with tennis balls, racket, drink, a towel, and in sunny weather a cap or visa. You might have an arrangement with your opponent as to who brings the balls;
• wear the appropriate shoes and sensible clothing. You will need to be aware of any club rules regarding attire, particularly if you are playing on indoor surfaces;
• prior to the knock-up, spin your racket or toss a coin to see who has choice. Remember, the winner can elect to serve, receive, choose an end, or ask his or her opponent to select one.

During the game
Ball management
• start with two balls near you, either one in your hand and one in your pocket, or one in your hand and one in your ball shorts;
• if the server needs a ball, the person nearest to the ball should retrieve it and pass it to the server;
• when sending the ball to your opponent, try to pass the ball carefully so that he or she can catch it after one bounce. Don't irritate your opponent by expecting him or her to run around collecting balls.

If you are fortunate enough to have line judges you must respect their decisions.

Line calls
• on the return of serve call the ball "out" before you return it, if you are going to hit it back to the other end;
• call the lines clearly and loudly so that your opponent can hear you. This will avoid confusion and hopefully prevent debate over line calls. You should only call a ball out if you are absolutely certain about the call;
• respect the line calls of your opponent and do not argue with them;
• if there is any degree of doubt, then a let should be played. This should not occur if only certain calls are made;
• if the match has an umpire, line-call decisions will lie with them. The decision of the umpire is always final, so arguing will only cause an awkward atmosphere;
• when playing doubles, you may find that it is easier for your non-serving partner to call the service line. It is best not to undermine your partner's calls.

Distractions
- ensure you put all your kit to the side of the court so it does not interfere with play;
- if you have booked a court but the previous players have not quite finished, stay clear of the court until your allotted time arrives. Remember that you would be annoyed if other players distracted you at the end of a match;
- never walk behind another court when a point is in play. Wait until the end of the point and then cross quickly;
- if standing or waiting near a court, talk quietly so you do not disturb the players;
- if a ball comes across from a neighboring court, wait until the end of the point before passing it back.

Body language
- try and appear positive, even if you are playing badly;
- avoid making exaggerated gestures when you win or lose a point;
- be mature in your reactions. This will help you to avoid creating a tense or argumentative atmosphere.

Playing as part of a team
- if you are involved in a team tournament it is expected that you are supportive and respectful toward your team members—even if you disagree with them at times;
- when playing with a doubles partner, be supportive and encouraging. Never criticize—after all, you are on the same side.

Tennis, with its element of both **individual and team competition**, offers great opportunities to turn rivalries into hopefully longlasting friendships.

> **HINT**
>
> The unofficial rules of tennis are as important as the official rules, and if the game is played in the right spirit it will be enjoyed by all. You will also have many more practice partners.

TURNING PROFESSIONAL

To become a professional tennis player is very different from enjoying tennis as a hobby or social sport. It is a long journey, and there will be many ups and downs along the way. There will be times when everything is going well, when you are making good progress and winning matches. There will also be times when you have setbacks because of injury, or loss of form or confidence.

Training hours

According to research into sporting excellence by Istvan Balyi (expert in long-term athlete development and training plans), it takes about 10,000 hours of training from starting the game to making the grade at professional level. You will need to be strict about your dedication to practice.

Ten year olds
Players should be training for 12 hours per week. This would be broken down to:
• 4.5 hours technical and tactical training;
• 2 hours coordination work;
• 1.5 hours speed work;
• 4 hours off-court practice (which at this age would include other sports and flexibility).

Twelve year olds
Training should be increased to 18 hours per week, composed of:
• 7.5 hours technical and tactical training;
• 2 hours coordination;
• 2.5 hours speed work;
• 1 hour strength;
• 1 hour endurance;
• 1.5 hours flexibility;
• 2.5 hours other sports and some mental training built into all the activities.

Fourteen-year-old females or fifteen-year-old males
Training should be increased to about 24 hours per week. These training hours would include tennis, practice matches, physical work, and other sports:
• 12 hours technical and tactical training;
• 1 hour coordination;
• 3 hours speed work;

• 3 hours strength;
• 2 hours endurance;
• 1.5 hours flexibility;
• 1.5 hours other sports.

Fifteen-year-old females or sixteen-year-old males
Training hours should be increased to about 27 hours. The breakdown would include:
• 14 hours technical and tactical training;
• 1 hour coordination;
• 2.5 hours speed work;
• 4 hours strength;
• 2 hours endurance;
• 2 hours flexibility;
• 1.5 hours other sports.

Sixteen-year-old females or seventeen-year-old males
Training hours should be increased to about 30 hours per week. This would include:
• 17 hours technical and tactical training;
• 1 hour coordination;
• 2 hours speed work;
• 3.5 hours strength;
• 2.5 hours endurance;
• 2 hours flexibility;
• 2 hours other sports.
   The top players at this stage will be traveling around the world playing European Tennis Association (ETA) tournaments or International Tennis Federation (ITF) ones.

Sixteen to eighteen year olds
Players should be aiming for the "$10,000 events" and satellite tournaments. In reality, particularly in the female game, many players reach this "mini-professional" stage by the age of 14 years old. Females tend to mature earlier in their game, whereas males seem to emerge later in their teens.

Annual plans

If you were to reach professional level and play full time, you would design your own annual plan. This would revolve around preparation, competitive phases (when you have key tournaments), and periods of rest.

For the majority of us, the most we will aspire to is a good club, or county, district, or perhaps national level.

Still, in order to do this, not only do you need to want to work and be prepared to spend hours practicing, but you will also require the advice and guidance of a coach to assist you on your journey. Your coach will help you to plan long term, will set goals that you can achieve along the way, monitor and re-evaluate these goals, then set new ones. He or she will help you with ranking targets and a planned tournament program. He or she will look at your technical, tactical, physical, and mental goals and how these fit into the phases of the annual program—preparation,

The author, **Sue Rich**, working with a young tennis player in Cambridge, UK.

competition, and rest. Without planning, you will not have any direction or focus, valuable time may be lost, the program may not be specific to you, and you may get bored and lose interest in the game.

Preparation
This phase involves general preparation and specific preparation, and in total would last 4–12 weeks. During the general phase you may do technical changes and work hard on the physical aspects of tennis, while in the specific preparation you concentrate on the tactics and mental skills needed for matches.

Competitive phases
These are the optimum parts of your tennis year, where you aim to be at your peak of fitness and ability to succeed in your target events. For the top players, the key competitive phases would cover the four Grand Slam events: The Australian Open, the French Open, Wimbledon, and the US Open. For an emerging player, competitive phases would consist of the qualifying matches for such tournaments.

The rewards, for a few, are enormous. Multimillionaire **Roger Federer** holds aloft the US Open trophy.

Periods of rest
After a competitive phase is over, it is ideal to have a period of rest and reflection before working toward your next competitive phase.

Seek advice from a good coach to guide you along your journey to fulfil your potential—whatever that may be.

A GAME FOR LIFE

By now you should have a good understanding of the elements that will make up your tennis game:
- skills of the game;
- some basic tactics;
- some ideas on the mental side;
- guidelines for improving your fitness.

Now that you have this grounding, tennis can offer you many bonuses throughout the whole of your life.

Tennis is a fantastic sport for young children to get involved in:
- players can begin as young as four or five years old, because the game can be adapted to suit all sizes and strengths;
- tennis is a great way to encourage children to stay aware of their fitness and get regular exercise;
- it is an individual sport that works on self-discipline, yet also has a team element that can help develop teamwork skills;
- successful young players will be motivated by opportunities to meet other young players and play in tournaments away from home and even abroad;
- the focus of the sport helps children learn to be independent, make decisions, and cope with difficult situations.

If you are a slightly older individual, looking to begin playing in your 30s or 40s, tennis also has many advantages:
- keeping active is not only important for children but also for adults, and playing

Tennis is **fun at any age.**

The Seniors' Tour has created fun for spectators as well as a new lease of life for some older stars. Here Bjorn Borg, John McEnroe, and Jimmy Connors prepare to resume old rivalries.

tennis is a fun and accessible way to maintain a healthy level of fitness, even as part of a busy schedule;
• involvement in club tennis is a great way to meet people—particularly if you start higher education, move away from home, follow employment to a new place, or simply want to make more friends;
• all sports are a great way to increase your confidence by setting yourself goals and improving your self-awareness;
• as players get older, tennis is a game that can be combined with any educational situation—from school club level to university scholarship standard;
• there are numerous job opportunities through tennis such as playing professionally, coaching, tennis management, refereeing, and umpiring.
    Although it takes time to develop your skills, it is never too late to start playing:

• many people find themselves looking for a new hobby as they get older, and also when approaching retirement. It is possible to take up tennis at any age and still enjoy its active and social advantages;
• as an informal game, tennis can be adapted to suit anyone's pace, meaning that you can work within your own capabilities;
• nowadays, tennis clubs offer a huge variety of coaching options and tennis groups for all age groups, including older players. The excitement of traveling and playing in different countries need not be limited to early starters;
• veterans' tennis is an area of massive growth, meaning that the opportunity for lifelong players to continue their career into their old age is unlimited.
    People all over the world have had lifelong enjoyment from the game of tennis—so if you haven't already tried it, start today!

The pace of tennis may **change with age**, but not the fun or competitiveness.

HINT

"The only possible regret I have is the feeling that I will die without having played enough tennis"—Jean Borotra, who continued to play and take lessons into his 90s.

TENNIS TERMS

A

Ace: a serve that wins a point outright and that the returner cannot even touch with his racket

Advantage: the point score after deuce; advantage is awarded to the player winning the point after the deuce score

Approach: the type of shot that allows a player to move from the back of the court to the front of the court

ATP: the Association of Tennis Professionals, the body that organizes professional tennis for men around the world

Australian formation: a specific type of doubles court positioning in which the server and net player are on the same side of the court

B

Backhand: any stroke played to the left of the body (if right handed)

Backhand slice: a backhand stroke played with the racket across the body, with a high to low action imparting spin on the ball

Backhand smash: a variation of the smash played over the head or shoulder from the backhand side

Backswing: the take back of the racket prior to the forward movement and eventual contact with the ball

Baseline: the line at the back of the court

Blocked return: a return of serve using a shortened action instead of a full swing

Bounce smash: a smash played after the ball has bounced

Building shot: a type of shot played in a rally to help the eventual winning of the point; it will be a tactical shot and not necessarily the shot immediately prior to a winner

C

Changeover time: the time allowed at the change of ends

Chip and charge: another form of approach where a chipped shot is followed by a rapid advance to the net putting the opponent under pressure

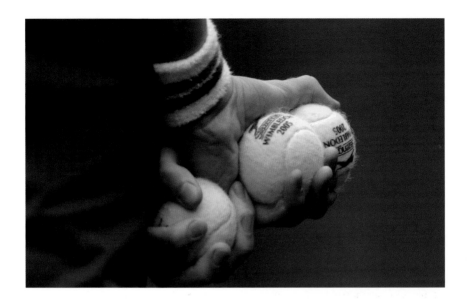

Choking: a term used when a player gets tight and nervous and misses easy shots and gives away points too easily

Chopper (grip): a type of grip used on the serve and, usually, when at the net

Closed racket face: when the racket face is pointing downwards slightly

Closed stance: a type of stance used normally on ground strokes when a player puts one foot in front of the other

Consolation event: when a player loses his or her first match in a tournament he or she can enter another event for players who have done the same (also know as plate event)

Continental (grip): another term for the chopper grip

Core stability: a term to explain the stability of the abdominal area which is valuable in playing good tennis shots

Counterpuncher: a style of player usually a defensive baseliner who reacts to their opponent's style of play

Cross court: the direction of the ball angled from one side across to the other; the opposite of down the line

Cyclops: the nickname for a device used to monitor whether the serve is in or out on the service line; it "beeps" when it identifies that a ball is out

D

Davis Cup: an international team event for men which is played each year, first in zones and then with a head to head final

Deuce: the score when both players have each won three points in a game

Double fault: the term used when a player has made an error on both his first and second serve, resulting in loss of the point

TENNIS TERMS

Drop shot: a delicate shot that is played to bounce very close to the net, normally played with spin

Drop volley: similar in intention to a drop shot (that is played to bounce very close to the net) but that is played before the ball bounces

E

Eastern (grip): the major forehand grip

End change: or "change of ends" when players change ends after the allotted number of games

F

Fault: and point-losing error but normally used when the server makes an error, hitting the ball wide, long or into the net

Federation Cup: known often as the "Fed" cup it is the major international team event for women, played annually with a head-to-head final

Follow through: the continuation of the stroke after hitting the ball

Foot fault: a point, or serve, losing error when the server's foot touches the baseline or the imaginary extension of the center mark before hitting the ball

Forced: a term normally referring to an error when the player tries too hard to hit a good shot and "forces" it

Forehand: any stroke played to the right of the body (if right handed)

Down time: time in between points and at change of ends, when no active play is in progress

Down the line: the direction of the ball hit from one side of the court to the same side in the opponent's court; the opposite of cross court

Drive volley: a ball that is hit before the bounce, normally played mid court and is a combination of a ground stroke and volley

Drive: the general term for a shot hit after the bounce (a bounce smash and chip shots, although hit after a bounce are not referred to as "drives")

G

Games: collections of points; a collection of games becomes a set

Go long: to "go long" implies a player has hit the ball beyond the baseline; it can apply to a serve going over the service line

Good return: a successful return over the net and into court

Grand Slam: the name given to four major annual tournaments: Australian Open, French Open, Wimbledon Championships and the US Open

Ground stroke: any forehand or backhand drive (not volley)

H

Half volley: a shot played just after the ball has bounced, struck immediately as it begins to rise from the surface

Hitting zone: the area of contact with the ball at the point during the swing in which the racket strings are facing where the player wants the ball to go (not to be confused with target zone or area)

Holding serve: when a player is able to win his or her own service games

I

I-formation: a specific formation in doubles where the net player is on the center line

ITF: the International Tennis Federation is the world governing body of tennis that aims to develop the game at all levels at all ages for both able-bodied and disabled men and women

J

Jump smash: a smash when the player has jumped off the ground to play it

K

Kick-back: the movement of the trailing leg as it is thrust into the air behind a player, normally on the serve

Knock-out draw: a type of tournament format where winners proceed and losers have no further part to play

Knock-up: the warm-up time prior to the start of the match when players knock balls back and forth to each other

L

Let serve: a service in which the ball touches the top of the net and then lands in the correct service box; it is not a fault and the server is then allowed another serve

Loading position: the power position on the serve when the left shoulder is higher than the right (if right-handed) prior to contact

Lob volley: a combination of a lob and volley when the ball is hit high into the air, played prior to bouncing

Lob: a ball which is hit high into the air

Looped preparation: refers to the take back of the racket in a "C" shape

Love: scoring term used to describe when a player has no points

N

Net cords: when the ball hits the tape on the top of the net

Net rusher: a player who tries to get to the net at the earliest opportunity

Neutralizing shot: a shot that makes it hard for an opponent to attack

O

On the rise: shots are taken "on the rise" referring to taking the ball on the way up after the bounce

Open Era: the period after 1968 when the game went "open": equally accessible to professionals and amateurs

Open racket face: the strings of the racket are facing slightly upwards

Open stance: a position adopted by the feet to hit a shot with the player's feet facing towards the net more than to the side of the court

Outright winner: a point-winning shot that an opponent does not get his or her racket to; an "ace" is an outright winner from the serve

Out: when the ball makes its first bounce outside the boundaries of the court

P

Passing shot: the ground stroke used to hit the ball away from an opponent at or near the net, played with the intention of passing them

Percentage tennis: playing the easiest or safest shot with the greatest margin for error in the hope that, eventually, your opponent will make errors

Plyometrics: a system of training that helps develop power, particularly useful in tennis where short-term explosive power is valuable

Poaching: when a player in doubles comes across the net and intercepts a ball that his or her partner could have hit

Progressive draw: a type of competition allowing players to move to parts of the draw where they largely play opponents of a similar standard

TENNIS TERMS

R

Rally: a sequence of shots played back and forth over the net

Ready position: the stance from which a player starts, prior to moving to the ball or contact

Real tennis: a traditional game (the forerunner of modern tennis) that is still played competitively on an indoor court with wooden rackets and a hard ball

Return: when the ball is hit back over the net, normally used to refer to returning the serve

Round robin: competition format when players are in groups and play everybody else in the group; winners progress to knock-out matches

S

Second serve: the second delivery of the serve, used when the first serve has been a fault

Seeding: a system of artificially placing higher-ranked players in a competition in such a place that they will only meet other "seeded" players towards the end of the competition

Semi-closed stance: when one foot is not completely in front of the other foot

Semi-western (grip): when the palm of the hand on the forehand is slightly under the racket

Serve-and-volley: a game style when the player serves and then immediately (or as soon as possible) follows the ball into the net in an attempt to play a volley

Serve: the act of striking the ball to start the play

Service box: the area into which the serve is directed

Service line: the line which forms the back of the service box

Sets: when a player has accumulated a certain number of games

Sidelines: sometimes referred to as "tram lines," these are the lines to the side of the court that form the boundaries of the singles and doubles courts

Slam-dunk smash: a specific type of smash when the player gets off the ground and tries to hit the ball down, hard into the ground

Slice: spin put on the ball that takes it laterally after the bounce

TENNIS TERMS

Smash: shot used to counteract the lob, generally hit hard with a powerful throwing action

Soft hands: describes a player's ability to play touch shots which require deftness and skill

Speed gun: a piece of equipment used to measure the speed of the ball, normally on the serve

Spin: the way a ball rotates in the air

Split-step: from the ready position a player will do a small jump in the air and land on two feet as his or her opponent strikes the ball; from here the player can readily move in any direction

Square stance: the position of the feet when you step with one foot in front of the other (not to be confused with stepping across)

Squash shot: a forehand drive, hit like a squash shot, with a slicing action

Stop volley: a ball hit before the bounce so that the pace is taken off the ball and it stops dead

Swiss ball: a large, training ball used to help core stability

T

Take back: how the racket is taken back after it has made contact with the ball

Taking the ball early: when the ball is hit on the rise, soon after or at the top of the bounce

Tie-break: scoring system used to end the set when it is six games all

Topspin: method of making the ball rotate forwards

Touch shot: a delicate or soft shot played around the net

Tramline: lines (sidelines) at the side of the court

Two-handed backhand: stroke played with the racket across the body with two hands gripping the racket

Two-way draw: type of tournament format where losers are able to continue playing more rounds

U

Unforced (error): an error made when not under any pressure and which should have been a routine shot

V

Volley: a shot that is played before the ball bounces

Volleyer: the name given to a person hitting the volley

W

Warm-up: period used prior to a match to prepare, both physically and mentally

Western (grip): type of grip when the palm of the hand is underneath the racket

Wrong foot: type of play when a player hits the ball in such a way that the opponent has to switch from running one way to play the ball in the direction they have just come from

WTA: the Women's Tennis Association, the governing body of the women's game

INDEX

A

ace 32, 178
advantage 178
Agassi, Andre 12, 26, 87
All England Croquet Club 9
approach shot 103, 136, 144, 159, 178
ATP (Association of Tennis Professionals) 12, 17, 178
Australian formation 153, 178
Australian Open 9 ,11, 16, 40, 181

B

backhand 74–87, 106–107, 108, 110–111, 117, 125–126, 143–144, 178, 187
backspin 118
backswing 64, 66, 77, 104, 107, 112, 119, 121–122, 136, 178
bags 45
ball toss 90–91, 101, 132
balls 12, 14, 43
baseline 178
beginners 46–47, 139
body language 17
Boland, John 10
Borg, Bjorn 15, 24–25, 80
breaks and changing ends 35
Budge, Don 20–21

C

chip-and-charge 179
clothing 44–45
coaches and coaching 47–49, 171, 177
competitions and tournaments 9, 16–17, 36–39
concentration 167
confidence 164–166, 170
Connolly, Maureen 21
Connors, Jimmy 15, 23, 25, 80

contact point
  backhand 78, 82
  drop shot 119
  forehand 68, 69
  lob shot 121, 123
  return of serve 105, 107
  serve 88, 92, 95, 97, 132
  smash shot 115–117, 137
  squash shot 128
  volley 110, 111
Cooper, Charlotte 10
coordination chain 89, 101, 132
court, dimensions of 31
Court, Margaret 22
Cyclops 12, 179

D

Davis Cup 11–12, 17, 179
deuce 34, 179
Doherty, Laurie 10
double fault 32, 179
doubles 152–155
drills 54–59, 130, 140–145
drive volley 180
drop shot 113, 118–119, 180

E

Edberg, Stefan 11
Emerson, Roy 21
equipment 14–15, 42–43
errors 150, 187
etiquette 172–173
Evert, Chris 23, 80

F

faults 31, 180
Federation Cup, The 12, 17, 180

INDEX